Maintain and Repair
Your
Computer Printer
and Save a Bundle

This book is dedicated
to my wonderful wife Kathleen.
Without her support, encouragement, and patience,
this book would have been possible—
but not nearly worth the trouble.

Maintain and Repair Your Computer Printer and Save a Bundle

Stephen J. Bigelow

Windcrest®/McGraw-Hill

Trademarks/Notices

Centronics® Centronics Corp.
LaserJet® Hewlett-Packard Co.
PostScript® Adobe Systems, Inc.
IBM PC® International Business Machines Corp.
Clean-A-Platen® Lee Products Co.
Solvene® Stanford Corp.

FIRST EDITION
THIRD PRINTING

© 1992 by **Windcrest Books**, an imprint of TAB Books.
TAB Books is a division of McGraw-Hill, Inc.
The name ''Windcrest'' is a registered trademark of TAB Books.

Library of Congress Cataloging-in-Publication Data

Bigelow, Stephen J.
   Maintain and repair your computer printer and save a bundle / by
Stephen J. Bigelow.
     p. cm.
   Includes index.
   ISBN 0-8306-2563-1 ISBN 0-8306-3507-6 (pbk.)
   1. Printers (Data processing systems)—Maintenance and repair.
I. Title.
TK7887.7.B54 1991
681'.62—dc20   91-24465
                                                CIP

TAB Books offers software for sale. For information and a catalog, please contact
TAB Software Department, Blue Ridge Summit, PA 17294-0850.

Acquisitions Editor: Roland S. Phelps
Book Editor: Susan J. Bonthron
Director of Production: Katherine G. Brown
Book Design: Jaclyn J. Boone
Managing Editor: Sandra L. Johnson
Cover Design: Sandra Blair Design and Brent Blair Photography,
  Harrisburg, PA   EL1

Contents

Acknowledgments

I would like to offer special thanks to NEC, Hewlett-Packard, and B + K Precision for their generous permission to reprint photographs and illustrations.

I would also like to thank my colleagues and friends at the Millipore Corporation for their interest and support during the development of this book. It made things a lot easier.

Introduction

Computer printers have rapidly become an indispensable part of the high-tech revolution. It seems that just about anyone who owns a personal computer has some sort of printer on hand, or has access to one. Their selection of style, size, shape, speed, and technology is enough to stagger the imagination. Each different model sports a variety of features and options. Their relatively low cost and flexibility have made a place for printers from the head office to the home office. Manufacturers have made printers readily available from almost every home electronics store.

In spite of their wide availability, the task of keeping a printer running properly is left solely to the printer's owner—often an individual with little technical training, few tools, and no repair information. As qualified repair services become more scarce (and inevitably more expensive), personal knowledge of printers and their repair techniques can save quite a bit of money.

About this book

This is a maintenance and repair book written for the novice. It is intended to provide nontechnical readers with a hands-on introduction to the principles, components, and operations of major printers. Chapters 1 and 2 review typical operations, specifications, technologies, and components found in most printers. Chapter 2 also covers communication standards and explains their importance. Chapter 3 offers a series of proven guidelines to follow in printer troubleshooting and repair. Chapter 4, 5, 6, and 7 thoroughly review the four central sections of every type of printer, with emphasis on common maintenance and repair problems. Chapter 8 concludes this book with a series of routine maintenance procedures that will keep printers running longer. Troubleshooting procedures are divided into three difficulty levels:

○ Level 1—Easy   No technical skill or special tools required.
◐ Level 2—Moderate   Simple tools required. Some technical aptitude helpful.
● Level 3—Hard   Simple test instruments required. Technical aptitude preferred but not essential.

Every effort has been made to prepare a clear and thorough book on basic printers. It is intended to be a general guide for the beginner, as well as a reference book for the nontechnical reader. For more technical information and procedures, refer to the book *Troubleshooting and Repairing Computer Printers* (Windcrest #3923). Questions, comments, and suggestions about this book are welcome at any time. Feel free to address any correspondence to:

Stephen J. Bigelow
Dynamic Learning Systems
P.O. Box 805
Marlboro, MA 01752

Doing the repair yourself

Stop for a moment and consider the computer printer in your office or den. Is it working properly right now? Is the print straight, crisp, and clear? Does the paper sag or tear as it feeds through the printer mechanism? Is it communicating correctly with its host computer?

Chances are that your answer to these questions is "yes." My experience has been that most commercial computer printers, regardless of their technology or options, will perform well through years of normal use. Like most other machines, however, your printer is going to encounter problems sooner or later. When your printer finally does need service, will you know what to do? Will you know what to look for? You could save a lot of money and time if you could repair your own printer.

If the word *troubleshooting* sends a chill down your spine, or the thought of disassembling that printer on your workbench makes your head spin, don't panic! Many printer problems can be corrected quickly with careful cleaning or some minor adjustments. This book will show you how various types of printers work, and what their components are. You will see each major section of the printer in detail, along with its typical problems and solutions. You will learn about routine maintenance. There are even procedures to follow if your printer needs intensive care.

Printer repairs are not as difficult as you might think. After you have read through the book and familiarized yourself with your particular type of printer, just roll up your sleeves and keep this book handy for quick reference. It will not be long before you can maintain and repair your computer printer and save a bundle.

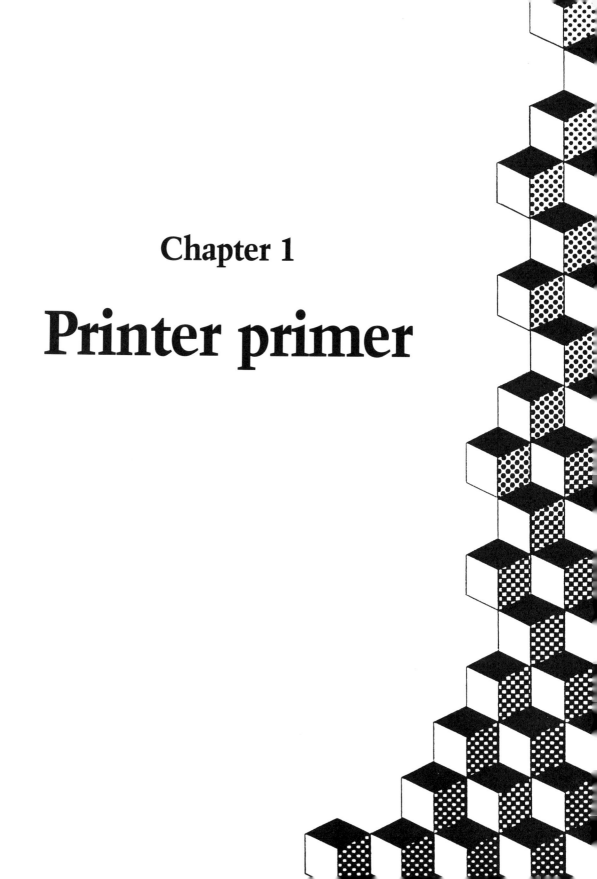

Chapter 1

Printer primer

A printer is a device used to record the output of a computer in a permanent form. Although this is a simple and straightforward premise, the actual process of transcribing computer-generated information onto paper is not easy. An assortment of electrical, electronic, and mechanical components (as well as optical and chemical components in some cases) work together to form printed pages correctly and reliably. Consider what capabilities typical printers, such as the ones shown in Fig. 1-1, must have.

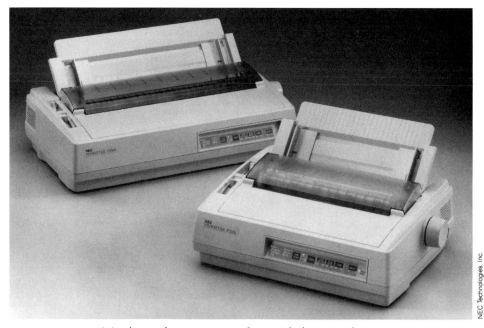

1-1   A set of contemporary dot-matrix impact printers.

What a printer is

Printers physically connect to almost any host computer. This connection, or *interface*, can be any one of several standard types. Some printers are compatible with more than one of these standards. (Chapter 2 discusses printer communication in detail.)

Printers work with a variety of different paper types. Most handle *tractor-feed* (or *pin-feed*) paper, but more printers are becoming available that handle single sheets of plain paper. Standard paper-handling mechanisms can handle paper widths from just a few inches to well over 9 inches. Wide paper-handling mechanisms can accommodate paper more than 16 inches wide.

This is standard Courier Font

This is standard Sans Serif Font

This is standard Prestige Font

This is Bold PS Font

This is 10 characters per inch (cpi)

This is 12 characters per inch (cpi)

This is 15 characters per inch (cpi)

This is 17 characters per inch (cpi)

This is Emphasized print

This is Double Height Print

This is Double Width Print

<u>**This is Underlined Print**</u>

This is Italic Print

1-2 Example of typical printer fonts and enhancements.

More than one type style, or *font*, is often available. Fonts are usually selected by special commands sent from the computer, through a control panel on the front of the printer, or by exchanging a font memory module in the printer.

Printers can modify fonts to provide such enhancements as italic, bold, underlining, superscript, subscript, double-high, and double-wide print. *Pitch* is the number of characters per inch (or *cpi*). A smaller pitch means that fewer characters can be printed per inch. Pitch settings of 10, 12, and 17 cpi are most common, but some printers can achieve pitches as large as 2.5 cpi and as small as 20 cpi. Figure 1-2 shows examples of typical fonts and enhancements.

After font, pitch, and enhancement characteristics are selected, printers generate the characters that are displayed on a page surface. Print speed depends on pitch and print quality, so a higher pitch or lower quality of print can display more characters faster than a lower pitch or higher print quality. Depending on the pitch,

1-3   Example of simple bit-image graphics.

print quality, and technology used, a printer can generate from 30 to 300 characters per second (*cps*).

Printers are not limited to printing characters. Many printers can generate graphics, often known as bit-image graphics. This allows printers to generate pie charts, bar graphs, or just about any other image. The *resolution* of the printer is the number of dots per inch (*dpi*) that a printer is generating. Simple dot-matrix printers can support bit-image graphics at as low as 60 dpi. This is often adequate for basic graphs or other simple printing jobs. More sophisticated printers are able to support resolutions at more than 300 dpi. Printers used for desktop publishing usually use this resolution for fine detail. Figure 1-3 is an example of bit-image graphics at about 80 dpi.

Not only is a typical printer capable of these things and more, but the printer must operate reliably for millions of characters under a wide range of temperatures, humidity levels, and locations.

With all of this to consider, you can understand why there is more to a printer than is seen at first glance. The following section shows you the technologies that printers use to accomplish their tasks.

Printer technologies

Since the early days of computer printers, manufacturers have utilized advances in chemistry, electronics, optics, and related fields to improve the speed and quality of their printers. Original printers worked much like the mechanical typewriters that our grandparents might have used, but it did not take long to incorporate smaller, lighter mechanical components, as well as integrated circuits, to reduce their size while improving their speed and reliability. Manufacturers also branched out to refine other printing methods using heat, ink, and light. This constant development and improvement has led to the four major printing technologies discussed in the next sections. These printing technologies are called thermal, inkjet, and electrostatic. Each of these methods is detailed in chapter 4.

Impact printing

The technique of *impact printing* is just as the name implies; characters (or graphics) are physically struck onto a page through an inked ribbon. Two types of impact printers are *character* and *dot matrix*.

Character printers are basically unchanged from the very first typewriters ever made. A set of alphanumeric characters is molded onto a support structure, or *die*. The die can contain any combination of upper- and lowercase letters, numbers, or special symbols. Fonts are defined by the shape of the molded characters. To change a font, simply remove an old die and insert a new one. Figure 1-4 shows a typical daisywheel die.

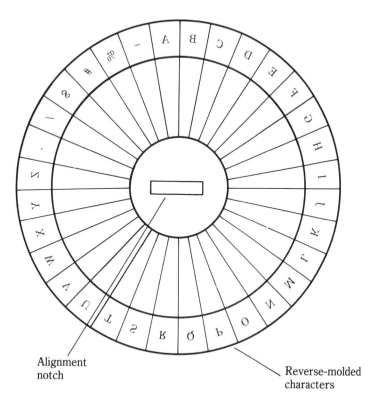

Alignment notch

Reverse-molded characters

1-4   A typical daisywheel die.

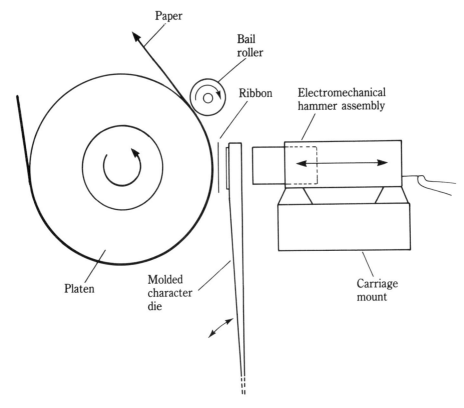

1-5   Character print head mechanism.

When a die is installed into a holder or print head, a signal from the computer causes the die to rotate until the desired character is facing the page. A striking mechanism, often called a *hammer*, then fires. Force generated by the hammer pushes the selected die forward against the page. This impact transfers the character image through an inked ribbon and onto paper. The entire print head assembly steps to a new position and another character can be printed. When the print head reaches a margin, the page is advanced by one line and the process is repeated. Figure 1-5 illustrates a character print head assembly.

Now character printers are essentially obsolete, due to two very important reasons. First, printing speed is limited because a die can only spin up to a certain rate. Second, character printers cannot print graphics or custom symbols—just the characters on the die. When you compare other printer technologies that can combine high-quality text and graphics on a single page, you can see why the demand for character printers has severely declined.

Dot-matrix printers have been around almost as long as character printers, but they have proven far more flexible. A dot-matrix print head uses a series of independent pins (or *print wires*) to strike the page as shown in Fig. 1-6. As the print head moves across the page, a vertical assembly of wires can be fired through an inked ribbon to form the desired characters. Because print wires can be fired in

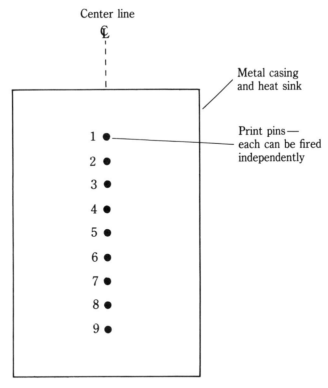

1-6 Vertical pin configuration of a typical dot-matrix impact print head—9-pin configuration.

any combination, it is possible to print more than one font style, as well as custom characters or graphics. Ribbons are typically black, but colored ribbons can be used. Multicolored ribbons are used in some impact printers to provide a range of colors on the same page.

Impact dot-matrix print heads typically hold 9 or 24 print wires. A 9-pin print head is an inexpensive, reliable workhorse. It can produce fair quality characters at a high speed, but it leaves a rough, dotted appearance as in Fig. 1-7. This low number of dots limits the number of fonts and enhancements that the printer can produce. To overcome this problem, manufacturers developed near-letter-quality (NLQ) mode that passes the head over the page several times to fill in characters. NLQ modes improved the appearance of print as shown in Fig. 1-8, but 9-pin print heads still appeared limited.

A 24-pin print head offers even more flexibility by providing two slightly staggered vertical rows of print wires as in Fig. 1-9. As a 24-pin head moves, it can place more than twice as many dots as the 9-pin head in each pass across the page. Figure 1-10 shows a single pass of a 24-pin print head. Notice that the characters are smoother and better defined. Additional wires also allow the printer to generate a greater range of fonts and graphics. Characters formed in NLQ modes, such as those in Fig. 1-11, are often comparable to those of character printers.

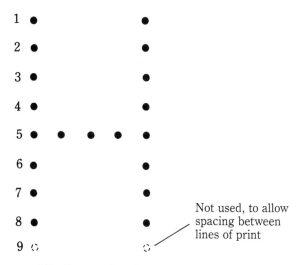

1-7 Dot-matrix print pattern—9-pin draft.

Impact dot-matrix printers are significantly faster than character printers. Speed can be enhanced tremendously since there are no spinning wheels or other large moving parts to wait for. High-speed dot-matrix printers can exceed 200 cps (when in draft mode).

In actual operation, computer data is translated into patterns that are used to fire print wires in their proper sequence as the print head moves across the page. Figure 1-12 is a diagram of typical dot-matrix print head assembly. Unlike charac-

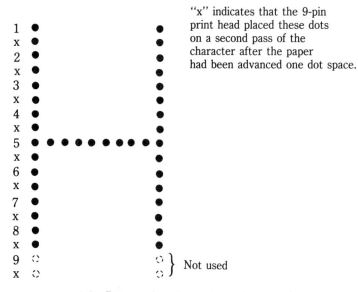

1-8 Dot-matrix print pattern—9-pin NLQ.

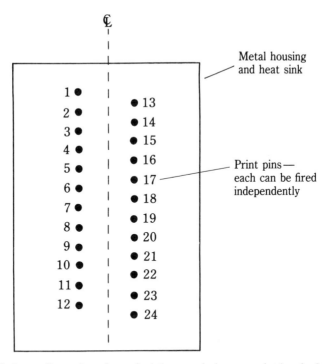

1-9 Vertical pin configuration of a typical dot-matrix impact print head—24-pin configuration.

ter printers, dot-matrix print heads do not stop between characters or columns of print. Wires fire while the head is continuously "on the fly." When a print head reaches a margin, paper will advance and printing will resume. Impact dot-matrix printers continue to be very popular for general-purpose use in just about any environment.

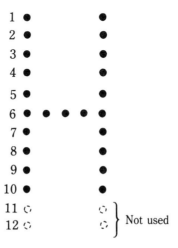

1-10 Dot-matrix print pattern—24-pin draft.

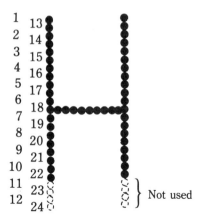

1-11 Dot-matrix print pattern—24-pin NLQ.

Thermal printing

Audible noise has always been prevalent in impact printers. The sound of dies or wires constantly striking paper can be obnoxious. In response to this complaint, designers developed thermal printing technology as an alternative.

While impact dot-matrix printers use metal wires to strike a page surface, thermal dot-matrix printers use dot heater elements molded into a solid assembly resting against a page. Electrical signals from the printer electronics will heat each

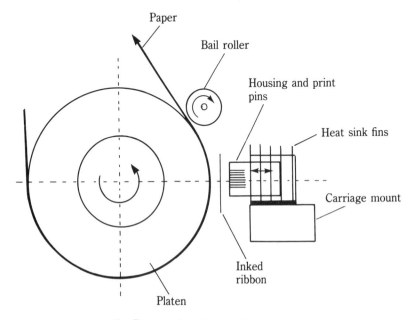

1-12 Dot-matrix print head mechanism.

dot in the proper sequence to form desired characters or graphics. Each heater is very small, so they will heat and cool again very quickly.

Normal paper will not work with thermal contact printers. Temperatures needed to color normal paper would burn it. Instead, a special paper is treated with heat-sensitive chemicals that will turn dark in the spots where dot heaters are fired. Print color is determined by the chemical composition used, but the most popular colors are black and blue. Unfortunately, thermal paper has two major disadvantages. First, it is a frail and delicate paper. Exposure to sunlight, heat, or certain alcohols will cause it to discolor. Second, images transferred to thermal paper are not permanent. Images will fade and discolor with time. In spite of these disadvantages, thermal contact printing has found acceptance. A popular application for thermal contact printing is in facsimile machines where their low power consumption and whisper-quiet operation are ideal.

Thermal contact print heads were originally modeled after impact dot-matrix heads as shown in Fig. 1-13. A vertical column of nine dot heaters were molded

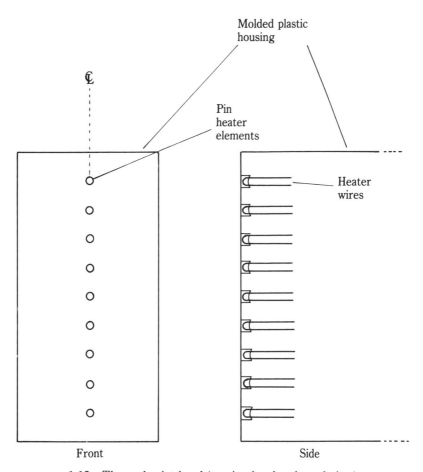

1-13 Thermal print head (moving-head, enlarged view).

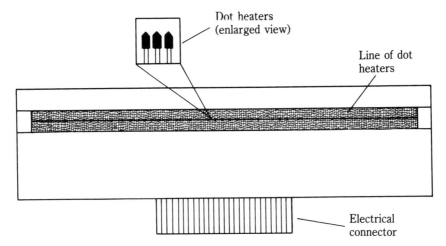

1-14   Thermal print head (line-head).

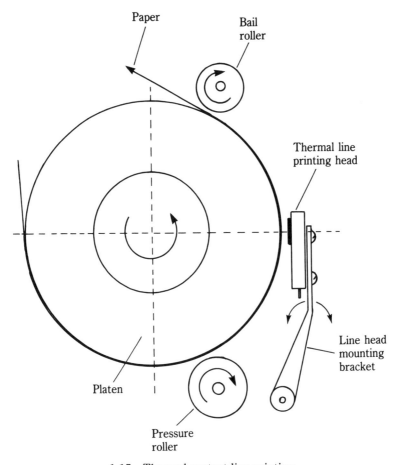

1-15   Thermal contact line printing.

into the assembly. The *heat sink* attached to the assembly was used to carry away excess heat. Operation of the thermal head largely resembled an impact dot-matrix head. Dot heaters fired as the head moved across the page, forming both characters and graphics.

Line printing uses a different version of the thermal print head. Instead of a small vertical column of dot heaters, a thermal line printer uses a complete horizontal row of dot heaters across the width of the page as in Fig. 1-14. The line printing method uses a stationary head to print one complete row of horizontal dots at a time. Figure 1-15 illustrates the thermal line printing technique.

Although the electronic circuitry needed to supply signals to operate a line printer is more complex than a 9-dot moving head, it offers the advantage of simplicity—fewer moving parts. The only moving portion of this printer is the thermal paper.

If a plastic ribbon coated with a dry, heat sensitive ink is placed between the thermal print head and print surface, heated dots melt the dry ink. Dots of melted ink are transferred to the page surface where they will dry quickly and permanently. This is the basic concept behind thermal transfer printing as shown in Fig. 1-16. The print head never actually comes in contact with the page. Thermal transfer printing may use either a moving or a line print head.

Any standard paper type can be used with this process because the thermal head is used for heating ink, not paper. Print color then depends on the dry ink

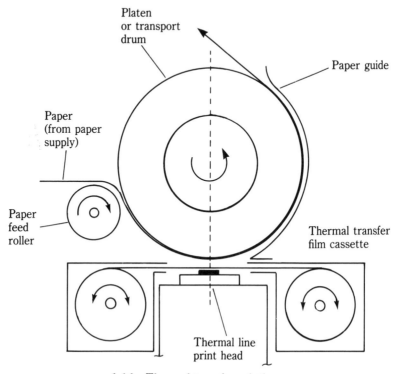

1-16 Thermal transfer printing.

color, so colors can be changed simply by changing the plastic ribbon. Some thermal transfer printers support multicolor printing by using ribbons with more than one color.

Ink jet printing

Ink jet printers offer fast, quiet, and flexible printing not only on paper, but on a wide range of printing surfaces. Look at your next soda bottle or soup can. Those long codes of letters and numbers that you see were probably applied using an ink jet printer. This is known as *noncontact printing*, since no part of the print head ever comes in contact with the surface to be printed. Characters, graphics, and special symbols are literally spray-painted onto the page from a reservoir of liquid ink. Although print is formed by a series of dots as in the impact dot-matrix approach, several unique methods are used to deliver the ink.

The *drop-on-demand* ink jet print head is shown in Fig. 1-17. This is the simplest and most widely used noncontact method for computer printers. A series of ink nozzles forms a vertical column on the face of the print head. Each nozzle is supplied from a central ink reservoir, usually located with the nozzles on a disposable print cartridge. As the print head moves across the print surface, control circuitry in the printer "squeezes" dots of ink as needed to form the desired print.

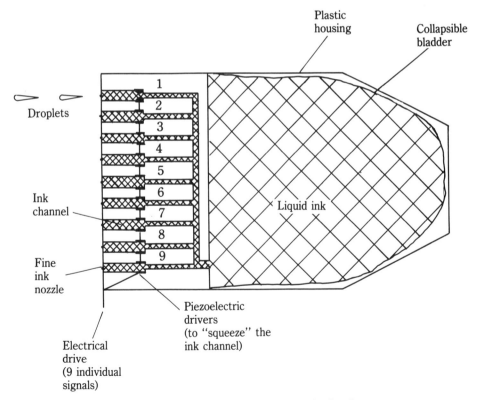

1-17 Ink jet drop-on-demand print head.

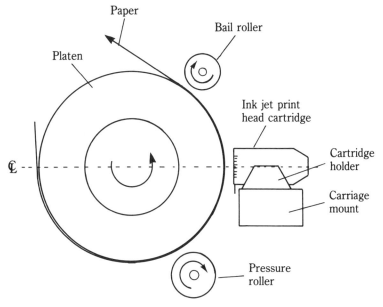

1-18 Ink jet drop-on-demand printing process.

Just how this is done is discussed thoroughly in chapter 4. Figure 1-18 shows a drop-on-demand ink jet print head assembly. Circuitry used to form dot sequences is almost identical for dot-matrix impact, thermal, and drop-on-demand ink jet printers.

Instead of squeezing out drops of ink with electrical signals, *bubble jet* printing uses dot heaters molded into the ink nozzles as shown in Fig. 1-19. A central ink reservoir supplies ink to all print nozzles. To fire a nozzle, an electronic circuit fires the nozzle's heater. The heater heats rapidly and forms an air bubble which expands in the ink channel. When the air bubble bursts, its force pushes a drop of ink out of the nozzle. The sudden vacuum pulls in more ink from the reservoir, and the nozzle is ready to fire again. Figure 1-20 shows a bubble jet print head assembly. The speed of bubble jet printing is limited, however, to prevent excess heat from drying ink within the nozzles.

Figure 1-21 illustrates a radically different approach used for *continuous flow* ink jet printing. A single stream of pressurized ink is broken up into droplets within the open print head. An electrical charge is applied to each drop as it passes through the head. This is a variable charge controlled by the printer's circuitry, which determines where the drop is to be placed. Each drop then passes through a set of plates holding a fixed electrical charge of an opposing polarity. Since opposite charges attract, the droplets are deflected out of the head to the page surface. If a drop is not to be placed, it does not receive a charge. In that event, the drop reaches a return vent where it is vacuumed back to a remote ink reservoir for reuse.

The pressure needed to push the drops across the nozzle to the page is much greater than in a drop-on-demand print head, where the nozzle is right next to the

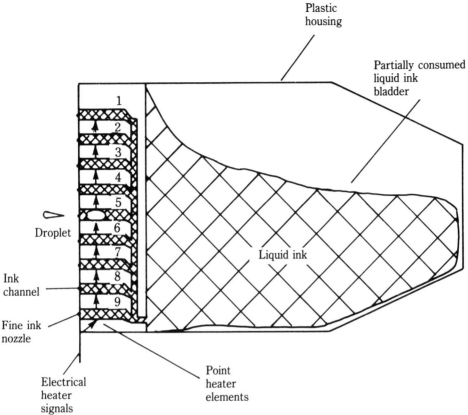

1-19 Ink bubble jet print head.

page. As a result, ink must flow quickly, but printing can be accomplished at speeds exceeding 60,000 dots per second (more than 1500 cps)!

This method of ink jet printing requires a source of air pressure and vacuum, as well as a large ink reservoir and a filter to clean recirculated ink before reuse. Continuous flow print heads must also remain stationary so ink will fly in a straight direction. Imagine what would happen to the flow of ink if the head were to start and stop like an impact print head. Ink would spatter everywhere within the head. To prevent this, the print surface must be moved in front of the head. This method of ink jet printing is used extensively for industrial marking systems where boxes, bags, or other packages are moved past the print head by conveyor.

Electrostatic printing

The process of electrostatic printing (ES) is not a simple one. An electrostatic printer requires the interaction of chemistry, optics, electronics, and mechanics to produce an image on paper. Although this technology has become well recognized since its introduction in the 1970s, the strict requirements and precise components needed to manufacture electrostatic printers have kept them delicate and expen-

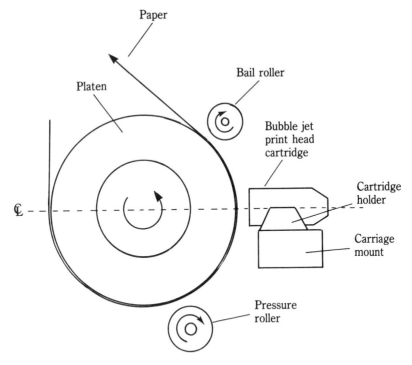

1-20 Ink bubble jet printing process.

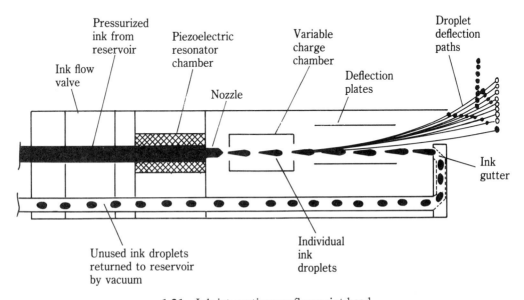

1-21 Ink jet continuous-flow print head.

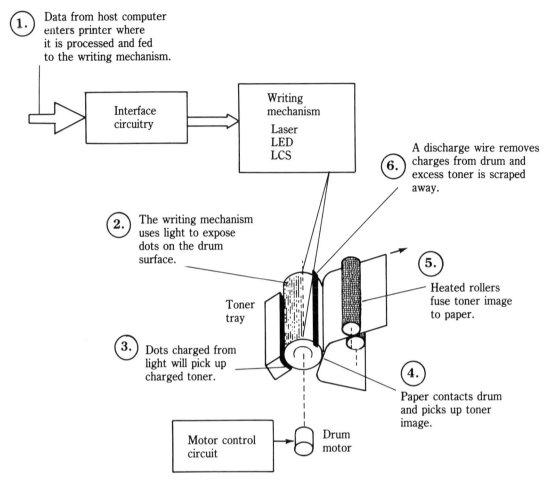

1. Data from host computer enters printer where it is processed and fed to the writing mechanism.

Interface circuitry

Writing mechanism

Laser
LED
LCS

6. A discharge wire removes charges from drum and excess toner is scraped away.

2. The writing mechanism uses light to expose dots on the drum surface.

Toner tray

5. Heated rollers fuse toner image to paper.

3. Dots charged from light will pick up charged toner.

4. Paper contacts drum and picks up toner image.

Motor control circuit

Drum motor

1-22   Generic electrostatic printer.

sive. There are three different approaches used for ES printing, but each works in a way similar to that of the generic printer shown in Fig. 1-22.

A precision metal drum is coated with a photoelectric compound of selenium. This coating develops an electric charge when exposed to light energy. Data from the host computer is translated into light data by the printer's interface circuits and delivered by a *writing mechanism*. The writing mechanism places the desired image onto the drum as rows of light dots. Lasers, light emitting diodes (LEDs), and liquid crystal shutters (LCSs) are typically used as writing mechanisms, and each is discussed in detail in chapter 4. When a dot of light strikes the drum, that point (and only that point) will take on a static electric charge. As one horizontal row of dots is written, a motor will advance the drum one small increment, and another row of dots can be written.

Toner is a fine granular compound which is easily attracted by a static electric charge. As the drum continues to rotate, it passes a reservoir of toner powder. Any areas on the drum that have been exposed to light and charged pick up and hold toner. Unexposed areas remain clean. A sheet of plain paper fed from the paper tray is charged by a high-intensity corona lamp and brought into contact with the drum. Toner is attracted off the drum and onto the paper. The printed page is then squeezed between two heated rollers which melt the toner image onto the page. Completed pages are fed to a paper output tray.

At this point, the exposed image must be removed from the drum to prepare it for a new page. To accomplish this, a discharge wire eliminates any charges on the drum as it passes. A scraper gently removes any toner residue remaining on the drum. The printer is now ready to print another page.

Lasers are the oldest and most established writing mechanism used in electrostatic printing. Laser printers can produce images with resolutions better than 300 dpi. The speed of a laser printer is limited by laser beam power because beam power affects how fast dots may be written to the drum. Simple laser printers might use a small laser diode, while a faster printer might use a more powerful gas laser.

Laser printers require a complex and delicate optical system to direct the beam precisely along the drum, as shown in Fig. 1-23. The mirrors and optics used in the assembly must be manufactured and aligned to exact specifications. Any irregularities result in dots that are distorted, out of focus, or out of line. This is the greatest detriment to laser printer reliability—if the optical system is knocked out of alignment, field repair is almost impossible without special optical alignment instruments.

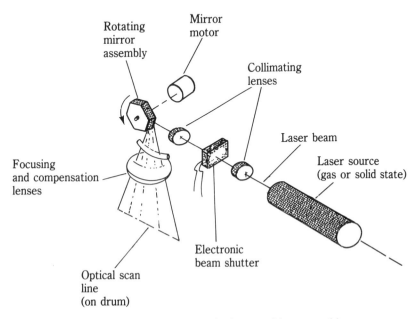

1-23 Simple diagram of a laser writing assembly.

Arrays of LEDs offer an intriguing alternative to lasers for speed, simplicity, and reliability. An LED array is essentially a row of small, individual semiconductor lamps—one for each possible dot in a horizontal row. For example, an LED array for a page 8.5 inches wide at 300 dpi would require 2550 individual LEDs in the row (300 dpi × 8.5 inches). This type of assembly is called a *print bar*. It is held in close proximity to the drum, as shown in Fig. 1-24. There are no moving parts or complex optics needed with an LED print bar, so reliability and ruggedness can be improved significantly. Alignment or replacement can be accomplished easily in the field.

LCS arrays offer the same advantages of simplicity and reliability. While LEDs generate their own light, however, liquid crystal arrays act as shutters to block or pass light generated by a long fluorescent bulb mounted behind the shutter array. Like LED arrays, there is an independent LCS for each possible dot in the line, as shown in Fig. 1-25. Print speed using LCS technology is slightly slower than the LED approach since the reaction time for liquid crystal material is slower than for LEDs.

Control circuitry for LED and LCS print bars is more complex than laser printers because each dot in the print bar must be controlled independently, but this increase in complexity is often balanced by their advantages.

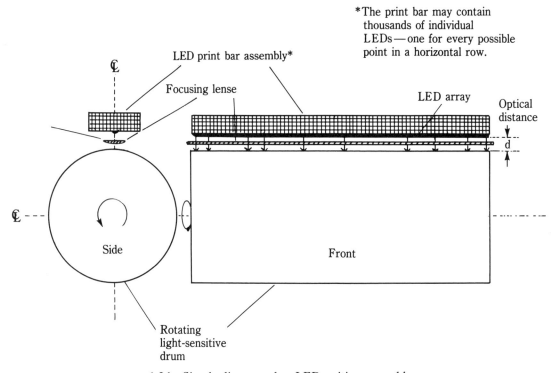

1-24 Simple diagram of an LED writing assembly.

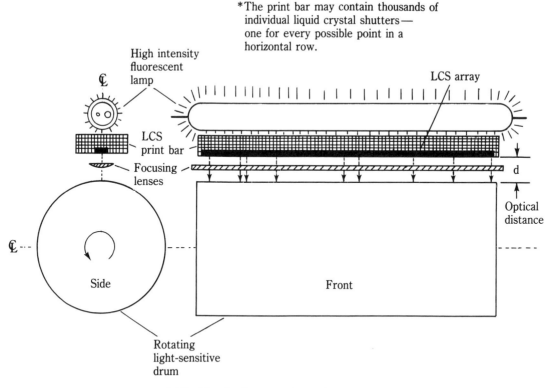

1-25 Simple diagram of an LCS writing assembly.

Understanding the specifications

When a printer is built, it must adhere to a particular set of operating specifications set by the manufacturer. These specifications summarize the most important facts of the printer's operation, including its power requirements, font styles and character sets, as well as printer life and reliability.

The problem with specifications is that no two manufacturers list the same specifications in the same way. There is no standard format or approach, so manufacturers can tell you as much or as little about their printers as they like. For the everyday printer user, technical specifications have little significance as long as the printer produces satisfactory results, but if you plan to repair a printer, it is helpful to understand fully the printer's capabilities. A listing of specifications is almost always included in your printer's user manual.

Electrical specifications

In order for the printer's electronics to function properly, it must receive an adequate supply of power from the ac line receptacle into which it is plugged. There are four specifications of interest here; voltage, current, power, and frequency. These are usually listed as *power requirements*.

Voltage is a measure of electric potential available to the printer. Domestic printers require anywhere from 110 to 120 volts. European printers need 220 to 240 volts. When the printer is actually turned on, it will draw current from the ac outlet. Just how much current will depend on the particular printer. Power is a measure of electrical work done versus time. It is the product of voltage and current, and may be measured as volt-amperes or watts. Frequency is the rate at which ac voltage will vary in amplitude, and it is measured in cycles per second (also known as Hertz, or Hz). Ac line voltage operates at 60 Hz in the United States, and at 50 Hz in Europe. Frequency is a fixed condition, so you never really have to measure it.

Under most circumstances, there is adequate power to operate a domestic computer printer from just about any 120 volt ac outlet, but if there is not, an otherwise operational printer may malfunction. You will learn the procedures for measuring voltage and current with a multimeter in chapter 3.

Electronic interface specifications tell you what type(s) of standard communication formats that the printer is compatible with. Most commercial printers are compatible with either the Centronics 8-bit parallel interface, or a version of the RS-232 serial interface. Some printers may be compatible with both interface standards. The concepts and operation of communication standards are discussed thoroughly in chapter 2.

Buffer size represents the amount of temporary storage memory that the printer has available to hold data being sent from the host computer. A larger buffer can hold more information than a smaller buffer. This allows a computer to send (or "dump") its information faster. It will then be free to work on other tasks. Buffer size is typically measured in terms of *kilobytes* (thousands of digital words), or K. Large buffers are measured in *megabytes* (millions of digital words), or Mb. For example, if your printer has a buffer of 8K, it will hold 8000 digital words.

Printing specifications

There are a variety of printing specifications that you should be familiar with before you begin troubleshooting. These outline the general speed and performance characteristics of the printer.

Printing fonts are the font styles that a printer is capable of producing. Remember that fonts are limited by the dot resolution of the print head assembly. Simple 9-pin dot-matrix printers offer fewer fonts than electrostatic printers. Resolution, also known as *dot pitch*, indicates the number of dots that can be placed in one inch of page surface. This too varies depending on your particular printer. It is not unusual to find printers with a dot pitch ranging from 60 to more than 300 dpi.

Print speed and *character pitch* are dependent on the font and print size selected. Print speed is defined as the number of complete characters (not dots) that are printed per second (cps). There are usually several entries for various font styles and enhancements. Print speed can vary from under 40 cps to 200 cps or more. Character pitch can be expressed as characters per inch (cpi) or characters per line (cpl), and can usually be entered through the printer's control panel or by special control codes sent by the computer. For example, a 10 cpi font will fit 10

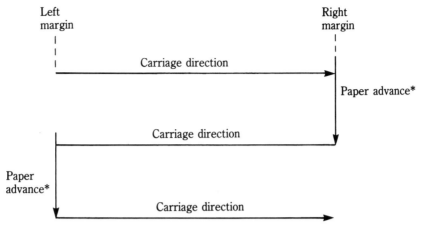

*Advance may be a full line or a micro-step
for NLQ printing

1-26 Printing directions—bidirectional.

characters in one inch. If the page is 8 inches wide, it will fit (8 inches × 10 cpi) 80 cpl. A 17 cpi font will fit 137 cpl in 8 inches, and so on.

Print direction applies *only* to moving-carriage printers such as a dot matrix. It does not apply to line or electrostatic printers. Most moving-carriage printers operate in a bi-directional fashion, as shown in Fig. 1-26. The carriage moves in one direction across the page, stops at the margin, advances the page, then moves across the page in the opposite direction, stops at the other margin, advances the page, then moves in the original direction. Everyday printing is usually accomplished

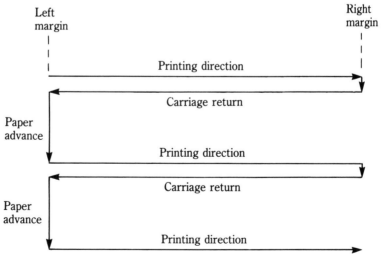

1-27 Printing directions—unidirectional.

this way. Unidirectional printing is shown in Fig. 1-27. The carriage moves across a page, stops at a margin, advances the page, then returns the print head to the original margin before starting a new line. Unidirectional printing is almost always done in left-to-right direction.

Reliability and maintenance specifications

You will probably be able to find specifications on print head reliability or expected mean time between failures (MTBF). Thermal and impact dot-matrix print heads will usually last for more than 100 million characters. A typical electrostatic printer should last for more than 200,000 pages as long as it remains in alignment. MTBF is a measure of reliability, but it is not published by all manufacturers. This figure represents the average expected time before a failure would be expected to occur under normal use. MTBF has nothing to do with the printer's warranty. It is simply a benchmark figure for expressing reliability.

Ribbon and ink cartridge life tell you how many characters or pages that the particular medium can supply before replacement. For an impact printer, this would be an inked ribbon. An ink jet printer would use a disposable liquid-ink cartridge. Electrostatic printers would use a cartridge of toner powder.

Tools and equipment

Before you attempt any type of maintenance or repair operation on your printer, consider the tools and equipment that you need to perform the procedure. First, you need mechanical tools for disassembly and reassembly of mechanical parts. It is a good idea to look over the printer carefully and anticipate any unusual or specialized tools that may be needed. A lot of frustration and wasted time can be avoided by gathering the proper tools *before* starting a repair. Second, you may need special cleaning materials, or test equipment to read electrical signals at key points in the circuitry.

General tools

For mechanical alignment and repairs, your toolbox should contain at least a selection of screwdrivers, pliers, and small wrenches. Figure 1-28 shows several common types of screws that you may encounter. Each type requires its own special tool. Unusual screws such as Spline and Torx are being used increasingly by foreign manufacturers to prevent disassembly by untrained personnel, but a large hardware store might stock these tools at a reasonable cost. Gather several small to medium sizes of screwdrivers. Needlenose pliers are preferable to standard pliers since they fit well into confined spaces. Small adjustable wrenches are handy for holding nuts while bolts are loosened or tightened.

Soldering tools

You will need soldering tools to tackle electrical repairs. A 25 to 30 watt soldering iron with a fine tip as shown in Fig. 1-29 is just right for delicate electronics work. Solder is the bright silver material surrounding the leads of each component on

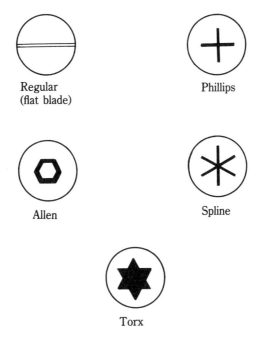

Regular
(flat blade)

Phillips

Allen

Spline

Torx

1-28 Screw head patterns.

any circuit board. When applied properly, it forms a strong electrical and mechanical bond between the copper in component leads and the copper traces of a printed circuit board. A bad solder joint will result in intermittent, unreliable operation. Use *only* rosin-core solder when working with electronics. Rosin fills the solder as in Fig. 1-30. This cleans the metallic surfaces to be soldered.

Before a new electronic component can be installed, the old one must be removed. This means that the solder holding it in place must also be removed. To accomplish this, you will need a solder vacuum or a length of solder wick. A solder vacuum (shown in Fig. 1-31) literally sucks molten solder away from the connection. Solder wick (shown in Fig. 1-32) is little more than braided copper wire. When it is heated against a solder connection, capillary action will draw melted solder into the braid. Appendix B reviews soldering and desoldering techniques.

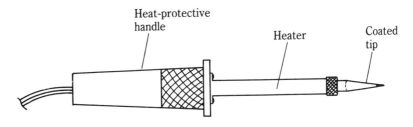

Heat-protective
handle

Heater

Coated
tip

1-29 Soldering tools—soldering iron.

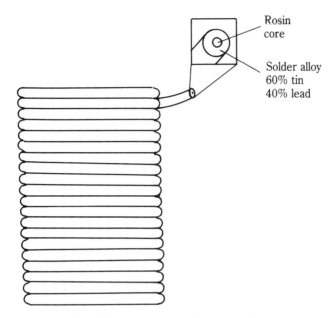

Rosin
core

Solder alloy
60% tin
40% lead

1-30 Soldering tools—rosin-core solder.

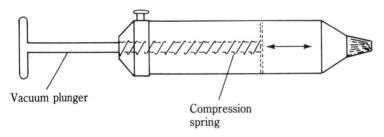

Vacuum plunger

Compression
spring

1-31 Soldering tools—solder vacuum.

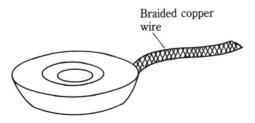

Braided copper
wire

1-32 Soldering tools—solder wick.

Test equipment

Unlike mechanical parts which you can observe easily, it is impossible to tell if electronic components are working just by looking at them. You need specialized test equipment to examine electrical characteristics such as voltage, current, resistance, and (occasionally) varying signal waveforms at key circuit points.

Multimeters are flexible and inexpensive instruments that can measure values of voltage, current, and resistance. More complex models can measure frequency, capacitance, and diode and transistor quality. It is this flexibility that makes multimeters ideal for most general-purpose circuit measurements.

There are two types of multimeters. Analog multimeters are generally a simpler and less expensive type. Test information is displayed by a moving needle in front of a calibrated scale as shown in Fig. 1-33. Digital multimeters use more sophisticated internal circuitry and are slightly more expensive. Test results are shown on a digital display as in Fig. 1-34. Since there is no scale to decipher, digital multimeters are easier to read and present fewer reading errors. This does not mean that they are any more accurate than analog multimeters—accuracy is a function of the meter's internal components. While multimeters are referenced extensively in this book, you should be aware of other available test instruments that can be used.

Logic probes are simple digital test instruments that display the level of logic signals or signal transitions in digital circuits. Logic states are usually indicated by colored LEDs as shown in Fig. 1-35. Your multimeter indicates a logic level by measuring its corresponding voltage, but a logic probe responds much faster to

1-33 Typical test instruments—analog multimeter.

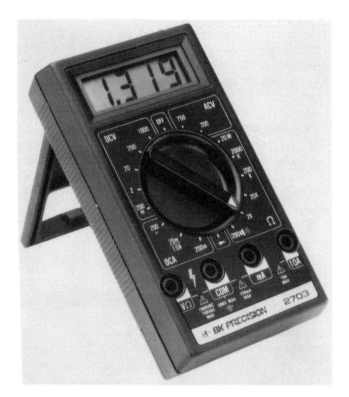

1-34 Typical test instruments—digital multimeter.

changes or repeating patterns in digital signals. This makes logic probes ideal for observing digital signals that are too fast or sudden for multimeters to "see" properly. It is worth the investment to have a logic probe in your toolbox.

Oscilloscopes (Fig. 1-36) are much more complex and expensive than multimeters or logic probes—but they are much more powerful. An oscilloscope displays voltages and waveforms on a video screen. It allows you to see precisely how digital *or* analog signals vary instant by instant. The visual representation can make any problem stand out. Do not be confused by the various settings and controls on an oscillocope. They are used only to change the way in which the oscilloscope "looks" at the signal so it can be displayed clearly. If you intend to use an oscilloscope, read the user's manual carefully and completely to be sure how each of the controls work.

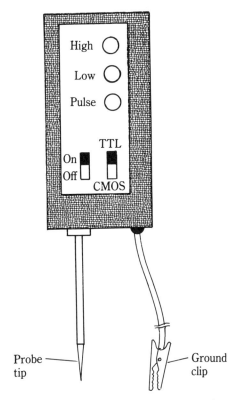

1-35 Typical test instruments—logic probe.

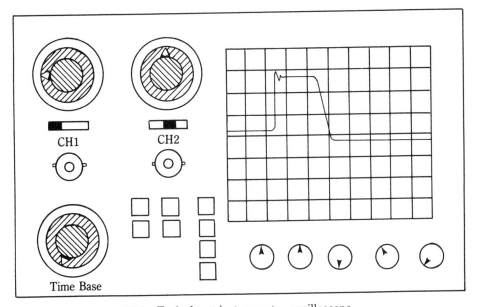

1-36 Typical test instruments—oscilloscope.

Chapter 2

Components and communication

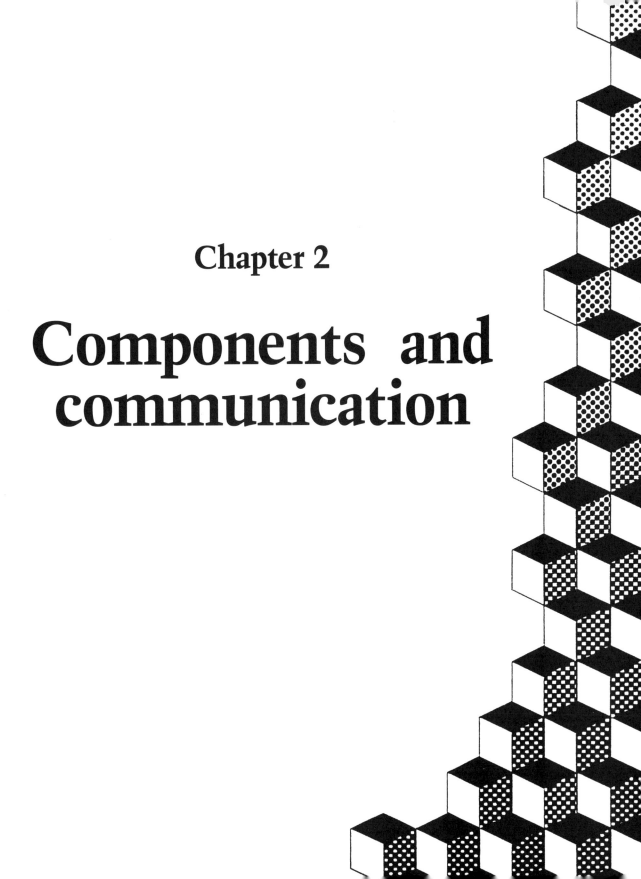

You should not be intimidated at all by the variety of technologies used in computer printers. While their size, shape, and speed may vary quite a bit from one model to the next, the same basic operational components and communication processes are required regardless of what technology is used. This chapter introduces you to the five functional sections in a printer. It also shows you the concepts of computer communications.

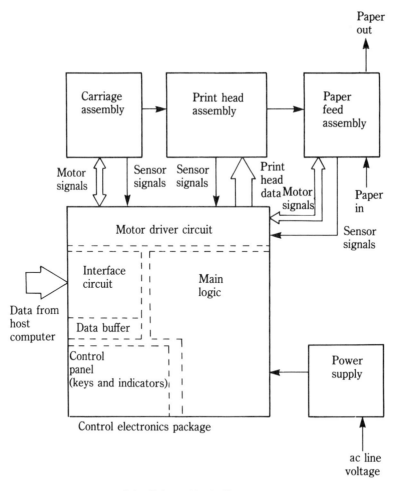

2-1   Printer block diagram.

Major components

Printers can be broken down into five operational areas as illustrated in Fig. 2-1. The *paper feed* assembly carries paper (pin-feed or single sheets) or envelopes through the printer. Print is physically delivered to the page surface by the *print head* assembly. Print head technologies were introduced in chapter 1. Printers with moving heads use a *carriage* assembly to transport the print head across the page. A *power supply* transforms ac line voltage from your wall outlet into voltage that the printer needs. An *electronic control package* communicates with the computer and controls the printer's operation.

Paper feed

There are two types of paper feed methods commonly used in printers. *Tractor feed* is probably the most widely used and easily recognized method as shown in Fig. 2-2. Continuous sheets of paper with holes perforated on both sides is threaded (usually from the rear or bottom of the printer) between the print head assembly and a hard rubber support roller called a *platen*. A platen not only helps to grip the paper as it advances, but offers some pliability for impact print heads

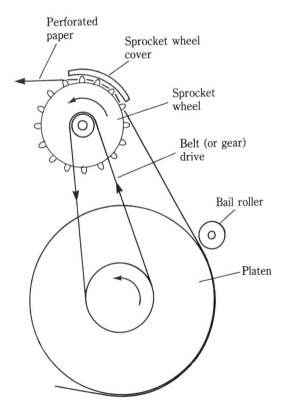

2-2   Paper feed assembly—tractor feed.

just like the platen of an ordinary typewriter. Rubber cushions the impact to ensure a smooth, consistent imprint.

A set of secondary rollers known as a *paper bail* will apply a small amount of pressure to paper against the platen. This helps to keep paper straight and flat in front of the print head. A set of sprocket wheels fit into the holes on each side of the paper. A belt or gear train connects the sprocket wheels and platen. After a line is printed, an electronic control signal will drive a feed motor to advance the platen. Sprocket wheels will simultaneously advance and pull the paper through by an equal amount. Since little pressure is applied to the paper and it is pulled through the feed path from the top, paper will remain very straight.

Single sheets of paper can be handled with a *Friction-feed* method as shown in Fig. 2-3. Paper is threaded between a platen and a smaller rubber *pressure roller*. After paper is loaded, the pressure roller is latched tightly against the platen which clamps paper firmly. When electronic control signals order a feed motor to advance the platen, friction exerted by both rollers will push the paper up through the paper path. A paper bail is still used to keep paper flat and even as it leaves the printer. This is the same technique used in just about every typewriter ever made.

Although friction feed is mechanically simpler than tractor feed, there are disadvantages that make friction feed undesirable. First, paper must be inserted into the feed path in a perfectly straight manner. If it is not, the paper will shift, or "walk" as it advances. Second, for paper to remain straight, the pressure roller

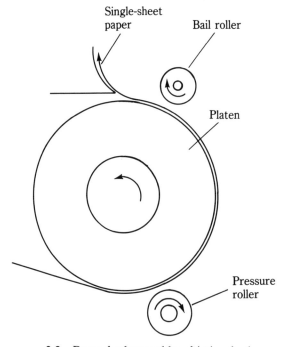

Single-sheet paper

Bail roller

Platen

Pressure roller

2-3   Paper feed assembly—friction feed.

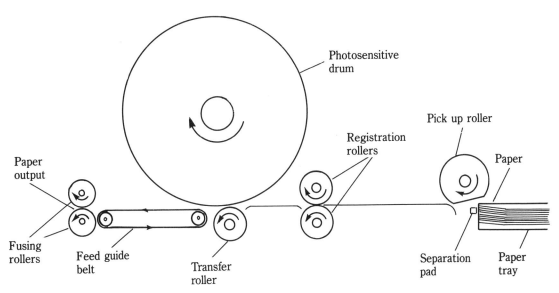

2-4 Paper feed assembly—alternate friction feed.

must not only apply pressure evenly over the entire platen length, but it must also be precisely parallel to the platen. Any uneven pressure or misalignment will cause the paper to shift and walk.

A paper feed method for electrostatic printers is shown in Fig. 2-4. You will notice that it is more complicated than other feed methods. A *pick-up roller* grabs a sheet of plain paper from a paper tray. The *separation pad* is little more than a rubber strip that applies friction to keep more than one page from entering the feed path. As a page is drawn into the printer, it stops at a set of *registration rollers*. These rollers hold the page stationary until the exposed drum has rotated to its proper position. When the drum is in place, these rollers start and feed the paper against the drum surface to transfer the toner image. A *feed guide belt* carries the page to a set of heated *fusing rollers* which melt the toner image to the page and feed it to an output paper tray. Chapter 7 covers the operation and maintenance of paper systems in detail.

Print head

The desired image of text and graphics is delivered by the *print head assembly*. An impact print head may use either a character or a dot matrix approach to imprint desired images through an inked ribbon. A thermal print head uses a dot matrix of small heaters to transfer images to a special heat-sensitive paper. Dots may be spray-painted onto a page with a noncontact ink jet print head. An electrostatic printing assembly transfers an image of charged toner to the page surface. Chapter 4 carefully examines each of these print head assemblies.

Carriage

When a print head must be transported back and forth across a page, a carriage is needed to carry it. Figure 2-5 shows a simple carriage mechanism. The print head assembly is attached to a steady mount which is free to slide along a set of parallel rails. Contact or optical sensors at both ends of the rails are used to limit the range of carriage travel. A *carriage motor* operated by the electronic control package drives a belt, wire, or chain which is fixed to the mount. As the motor spins clockwise or counter-clockwise, the mount (and print head) is pulled left or right.

It is imperative that the mount be free to slide without resistance. Any friction or interference results in uneven and distorted printing. Carriage troubleshooting and maintenance are covered in chapter 7. Routine maintenance procedures for carriage assemblies are discussed in chapter 8.

Power supply

Every printer has a power supply which converts home or office wall voltage into the various voltage levels needed by motors and electronic circuitry in the printer. Exactly which voltage levels are produced depends on the needs of each particular printer model and the technology used. Chapter 5 provides a complete discussion of power supply operation and maintenance.

Electronic control package

Printers are controlled by electronic circuits. While the amount and complexity of control circuits varies depending on the particular features and options of the

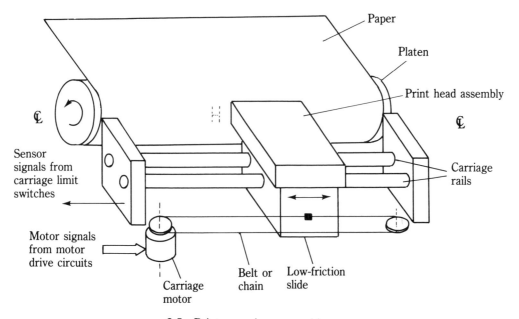

2-5   Printer carriage assembly.

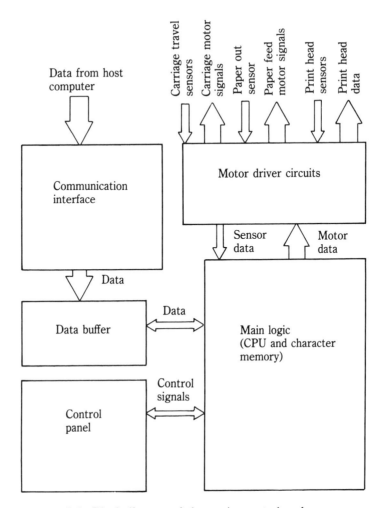

2-6 Block diagram of electronics control package.

printer, all electronic control packages have the same five basic circuit sections shown in Fig. 2-6, a communication interface, a data buffer, main logic, motor drivers, and a control panel (keyboard and displays).

Interface circuitry handles communication between the printer and host computer. Character and control data can be transferred in either *serial* and *parallel* form. A computer sends serial data one piece at a time. When the required number of pieces are received, one complete *word* is formed which is then stored in a data buffer. This word can represent a letter, number, symbol, or control code. Since all data travels in series, only one wire is needed to carry it. Parallel communication transfers all pieces of a word together. This is faster, but a separate wire is needed to carry each piece of a word. As a result, parallel printer cables are more complicated than serial cables. Parallel words can also be stored immediately in the data buffer since they do not have to be reassembled from serial pieces first. Communication standards and operations are discussed later in this chapter.

A computer can send data much faster than any printer is capable of printing. By adding a section of temporary storage memory known as a *data buffer*, the computer can send data in a burst, wait for the computer to print the data, then send another burst. This process continues until every needed piece of data is transferred. Just how long a computer must be involved in this process depends on the printer's speed and buffer size. A faster printer with a large buffer accepts data sooner, freeing the computer to perform other operations.

The *main logic* circuit processes all data sent from the computer and supervises the printer's overall operation. It processes information from the data buffer and generates control signals for carriage, paper-feed, and print head operation. Main logic translates data from the buffer into die position information, or dot patterns for characters and graphics that are delivered to the page. Various sensors report to the main logic about such factors as paper presence, print head temperature, or carriage travel limits. As printers become more sophisticated, control logic becomes more powerful and complex.

Although main logic circuits generate control signals for the motors, relays, or solenoids that might be in the printer, digital logic cannot operate these devices directly. Additional heavy-duty circuitry is needed to condition the control signals. These *driver* components take low-power digital signals and convert them into high-power signals that operate electromechanical devices. Electrostatic printers need driver circuits to operate a drum motor, mirror rotation motor (for laser printers) and a paper feed motor. Moving head printers need circuits to drive a carriage motor, and platen/paper feed motor. Even line printers that do not need a carriage require circuitry to run a paper advance motor.

A *control panel* allows the operator to enter such parameters as font type, characters per inch, or other enhancements right at the printer. Indicator lamps such as light emitting diodes (LEDs) display the operating modes that have been selected. Figure 2-7 shows a diagram of a typical printer control panel. Most printers also offer a "self-test" option, selected from the front panel, that tests print quality and consistency. Chapter 6 explains the detailed operation and repair of printer electronics. Electronic components are reviewed in appendix C.

Communication basics

A printer is a computer peripheral device—an extension of the computer. No matter how sophisticated your printer may be, it can do nothing unless it is specifically directed by the computer. In order for a printer to do anything meaningful, a communication link must be established between computer and printer. This is done by connecting a specialized cable between them. Before you learn the physical wiring and operation of the communication link, you must understand the type of information that a link carries.

Three types of information are sent to a printer: characters, control codes, and graphics data. Remember that graphics data are not accepted by all types of

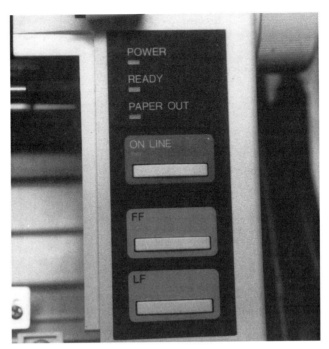

2-7 View of a printer control panel.

printers. Character data can represent letters (in any language), numbers, punctuation, or other symbols that appear on the page. Control codes are used to send commands to the printer. They can set such general things as font style, enhancements, or cpi, as well as immediate operations like line or form feed. When a control code places the printer into a graphics mode, it accepts graphics data instead of character codes. The difference is in the way data is processed and sent to the print head assembly. An opposing control code or reset command returns the printer to a character mode.

ASCII explained

Before any communication can take place, both the computer and printer must speak the same "language." In electronics, this language takes the form of a standard set of codes that represent some minimum number of characters and control instructions. In the early days of computers, each manufacturer had their own code set. You can probably imagine how difficult it was to combine equipment made by various manufacturers. The American Standard Code for Information Interchange (known as *ASCII*) was accepted to provide a single, common code set that all computers could use to transfer information. Figure 2-8 is a standard ASCII table showing characters, their code numbers, and the binary representation of their numbers.

The standard ASCII code covers letters (upper and lower case), numbers, simple symbols, and some basic control codes. For example, if you want a capital *D* to

Character	Code	Binary	Character	Code	Binary	Character	Code	Binary
NUL	0	0000 0000	+	43	0010 1011	V	86	0101 0110
SOH	1	0000 0001	,	44	0010 1100	W	87	0101 0111
STX	2	0000 0010	-	45	0010 1101	X	88	0101 1000
ETX	3	0000 0011	.	46	0010 1110	Y	89	0101 1001
EOT	4	0000 0100	/	47	0010 1111	Z	90	0101 1010
ENQ	5	0000 0101	0	48	0011 0000	[	91	0101 1011
ACK	6	0000 0110	1	49	0011 0001	\	92	0101 1100
BEL	7	0000 0111	2	50	0011 0010	]	93	0101 1101
BS	8	0000 1000	3	51	0011 0011	^	94	0101 1110
HT	9	0000 1001	4	52	0011 0100	__	95	0101 1111
LF	10	0000 1010	5	53	0011 0101	`	96	0110 0000
VT	11	0000 1011	6	54	0011 0110	a	97	0110 0001
FF	12	0000 1100	7	55	0011 0111	b	98	0110 0010
CR	13	0000 1101	8	56	0011 1000	c	99	0110 0011
SO	14	0000 1110	9	57	0011 1001	d	100	0110 0100
SI	15	0000 1111	:	58	0011 1010	e	101	0110 0101
DLE	16	0001 0000	;	59	0011 1011	f	102	0110 0110
DC1	17	0001 0001	<	60	0011 1100	g	103	0110 0111
DC2	18	0001 0010	=	61	0011 1101	h	104	0110 1000
DC3	19	0001 0011	>	62	0011 1110	i	105	0110 1001
DC4	20	0001 0100	?	63	0011 1111	j	106	0110 1010
NAK	21	0001 0101	@	64	0100 0000	k	107	0110 1011
SYN	22	0001 0110	A	65	0100 0001	l	108	0110 1100
ETB	23	0001 0111	B	66	0100 0010	m	109	0110 1101
CAN	24	0001 1000	C	67	0100 0011	n	110	0110 1110
EM	25	0001 1001	D	68	0100 0100	o	111	0110 1111
SUB	26	0001 1010	E	69	0100 0101	p	112	0111 0000
ESC	27	0001 1011	F	70	0100 0110	q	113	0111 0001
FS	28	0001 1100	G	71	0100 0111	r	114	0111 0010
GS	29	0001 1101	H	72	0100 1000	s	115	0111 0011
RS	30	0001 1110	I	73	0100 1001	t	116	0111 0100
US	31	0001 1111	J	74	0100 1010	u	117	0111 0101
SP	32	0010 0000	K	75	0100 1011	v	118	0111 0110
!	33	0010 0001	L	76	0100 1100	w	119	0111 0111
"	34	0010 0010	M	77	0100 1101	x	120	0111 1000
#	35	0010 0011	N	78	0100 1110	y	121	0111 1001
$	36	0010 0100	O	79	0100 1111	z	122	0111 1010
%	37	0010 0101	P	80	0101 0000	{	123	0111 1011
&	38	0010 0110	Q	81	0101 0001	¦	124	0111 1100
'	39	0010 0111	R	82	0101 0010	}	125	0111 1101
(	40	0010 1000	S	83	0101 0011	—	126	0111 1110
)	41	0010 1001	T	84	0101 0100	DEL	127	0111 1111
*	42	0010 1010	U	85	0101 0101			

2-8 Standard ASCII table.

be printed, the computer sends the code 68 to the printer. The printer in turn would translate the 68 into the dot pattern that reflects the selected font, character pitch, and enhancements to form a *D*. To print the word *Hello*, the computer sends the following sequence: 72, 101, 108, 108, and 111. Notice that ASCII uses the numbers 0 through 127.

Due to the way that data is actually sent, most computers can also use codes ranging from 128 to 255. Remember that any code over 127 is NOT standard. This is usually called an *alternate character set*. An alternate character set might contain simple graphic characters, Greek symbols or other foreign language characters. In some cases, codes 128 to 255 just duplicate codes 0 to 127. If your computer sends a code from 128 to 255, you may be printing characters that are different from those seen on your computer screen.

Control codes

When ASCII was first developed, printers were primitive by today's standards. Multiple fonts and type sizes, graphics and NLQ modes had not even been considered. As a result, ASCII supports only a minimum of codes that control a printer's operation. You might recognize such commands as Form Feed (FF), Line Feed (LF), or Carriage Return (CR) from Fig. 2-8.

With the introduction of advanced electronic circuitry, a greater amount of "intelligence" became possible in printers. ASCII control codes are still standard for characters, but are no longer enough to cover the variety of commands that are needed. Manufacturers responded to this shortcoming by devising a series of multicode control sequences. These *escape sequences* are named for the ASCII escape code 27 often used as a prefix. Escape codes are NOT standard, so there are some variations between printers.

Escape codes are typically two or three ASCII codes long. For example, to set a printer to compressed print, a computer sends an Escape (the number 27) followed by SI (the number 15). Software contained in the printer's main logic circuit interprets the code sequence and changes the appropriate modes of operation. A typical sequence to set a new print pitch might be Escape followed by g. In ASCII, this is 27 followed by 103. Multicode sequence will certainly become more common as printers become even more sophisticated.

Number systems

Not only must the computer and printer exchange codes that they both understand, but every code must be transmitted in a number system that is compatible with electronic circuitry. You know the decimal (or base 10) number system. The symbols 0 through 9 are used in combinations that can express any quantity. The symbols themselves are irrelevant—ten other symbols could just as easily have been chosen, but 0 through 9 are the ones we have accepted through the centuries.

	10^5	10^4	10^3	10^2	10^1	10^0
Decimal (base 10)	100000	10000	1000	100	10	1
				2	7	6

$$2 \times 100 = 200$$
$$7 \times 10 = 70$$
$$6 \times 1 = 6$$
$$276$$

2-9   Number system example—decimal.

	2^7	2^6	2^5	2^4	2^3	2^2	2^1	2^0
Binary (base 2)	128	64	32	16	8	4	2	1
				1	0	1	0	0

$$
\begin{aligned}
0 \times 1 &= 0 \\
0 \times 2 &= 0 \\
1 \times 4 &= 4 \\
0 \times 8 &= 0 \\
1 \times 16 &= \underline{16} \\
& \quad\, 20
\end{aligned}
$$

2-10 Number system example—binary.

What *is* important is the quantity of characters in the number system. In decimal, one character can express 10 levels or magnitudes (0 – 9). When the magnitude to be expressed exceeds the capacity of a single character, the number carries over into a higher place that is equal to the base of the system, raised to the power of the place as shown in Fig. 2-9. As the figure shows, the number 276 has a 2 in the hundreds place, a 7 in the tens place, and a 6 in the ones place. You have done this since grammar school.

If electronic circuits could recognize ten different levels for a single digit, then electronics would be directly compatible with our human decimal system, and ASCII codes would be exchanged in a decimal form. Unfortunately, digital electronics can only recognize two levels of a signal. These conditions are interpreted as true/false or on/off. This is known as the *binary* or (base 2) number system. Since only two conditions can exist, the binary number system only needs two symbols to represent them. The symbols *0* and *1* are the commonly accepted digits. ASCII codes are sent as binary digits. Figure 2-10 shows a binary number. Notice how the weight of each place is now a power of 2 instead of a power of 10. Each equivalent weight where a binary 1 is used can be added together as shown (0's are ignored). Figure 2-10 shows that the binary number 10100 is equal to the decimal number 20. A lower case *u* with the ASCII code of 117 is transmitted as binary 1110101. This is a 7-bit code which can express decimal numbers from 0 to 127. An 8th bit is needed to express decimal numbers from 128 to 255.

Binary digits

Since electronic circuits in both the printer and the computer operate on voltages derived from their power supplies, there must be a direct relationship between a binary digit and a voltage level. Since a binary *1* is considered to be an ON condition, it indicates the presence of a voltage. A binary *0* is considered to be an OFF condition, so it describes the absence of a voltage.

Consider the simple circuits shown in Fig. 2-11 through 2-13. Figure 2-11 shows a circuit with its switch closed. This applies a voltage to the lamp. This is an ON state. Figure 2-12 shows the circuit with its switch open. Voltage is now

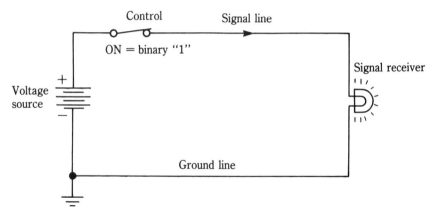

2-11 Simple binary circuit—sending a "1."

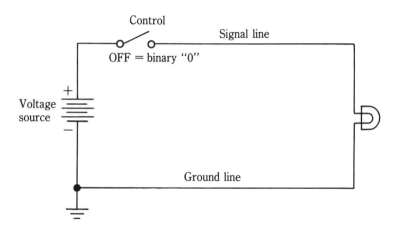

2-12 Simple binary circuit—sending a "0."

removed from the lamp, so it is in the OFF state. Figure 2-13 shows how each of these components relate to the link between computer and printer. The exact amount of voltage that defines an ON or OFF state will depend on the type of communication link established.

Parallel vs. serial

When ASCII or graphic data is sent to a printer, the binary digits that make up the word can be sent along either a *parallel* or *serial* communication link. A parallel link sends all bits of a binary word simultaneously over individual wires as shown in Fig. 2-14. A serial link transmits a binary word one bit at a time as in Fig. 2-15. Notice that both links are shown with a "ground" wire. Although only data leads actually carry information, the ground wire provides an important reference point between printer and computer circuits.

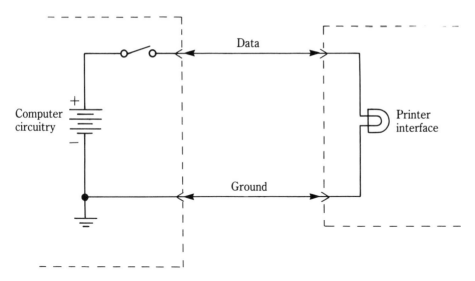

2-13 Simple binary circuit—a communication link.

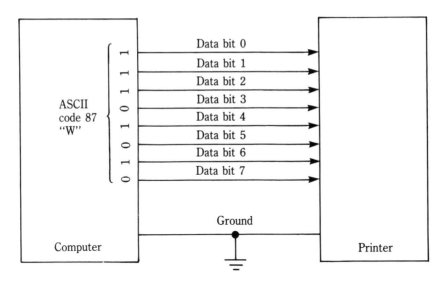

2-14 Communication link—parallel.

Parallel interface

A parallel link is the easiest to understand because of its straightforward operation. Figure 2-16 shows a simplified block diagram of a parallel interface. Notice that eight individual wires are used to transmit each bit of a binary data word together. Data lines alone, however, are not enough to transfer information successfully. Both the computer and printer must be synchronized so that the printer can accept data when it is offered, or ask the computer to wait until it is ready.

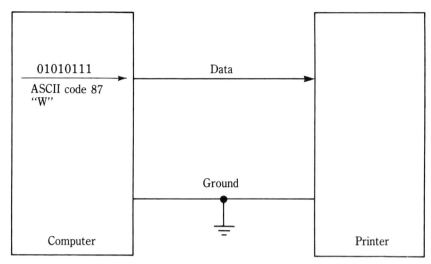

2-15 Communication link—serial.

Synchronization is accomplished using several control wires in addition to data lines. Some control lines signal the printer, others signal the computer. This process is known as *handshaking*.

In Fig. 2-16, if an 8-bit data word is sent, the computer places the word on data lines. It then sends a binary signal on a *strobe* line to tell the printer that valid data

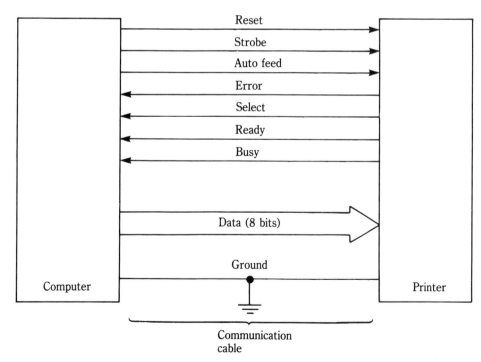

2-16 Generic parallel interface.

is available. The printer recognizes this strobe and stores the data word in its buffer for processing. While that word is being stored and processed, the printer sends a binary "busy" signal back to the computer. This asks the computer to wait until it is caught up. After data is processed, any busy condition is removed, and a separate "ready" signal, requesting another data word, is sent to the computer. The computer accepts a ready condition and sends a new data word if needed.

This is the minimum amount of handshaking needed to assemble a parallel interface, but there are often other control lines to consider. An *error* signal (usually a "paper out" indicator) is sent to the computer if the printer discovers an operating problem. A *reset* signal can be used to initialize the printer and clear its buffer. It is usually received when the computer is first turned on, but can be sent as a control code at any time during the printer's operation. A *feed* signal tells the printer whether or not to add a Line Feed character (ASCII code 10) automatically to any Carriage Return character (ASCII code 13) sent to the printer.

Parallel operation is reasonably fast. Some interfaces operate at speeds exceeding 1000 cps. At eight bits per character, that amounts to more than 8000 bits per second (bps). Parallel data can be stored in a data buffer directly, so parallel communication circuitry is often simpler than a serial interface. The disadvantage to parallel links is limited distance. With so many high speed signals running together in the same cable, its length is limited to just a few feet. This type of link is also unidirectional—data only moves from a computer to a printer. Only handshaking signals are returned.

Serial interface

Although a serial communication link might appear simple because of its reduced wiring, its actual operation is somewhat involved. Figure 2-17 shows a block diagram for a generic serial interface. Notice that two wires are used to transfer data. One of those wires sends data from the computer to the printer, while the other wire sends data from the printer to the computer. This is a bidirectional data link since data can be sent in both directions. With only one line available to send (or receive), data must be sent one bit at a time. Serial data must also be synchronized between the computer and printer. To accomplish this over a single wire, synchronization bits are added at the beginning and end of the serial data stream. An additional bit (known as a "parity" bit) might also be added to allow error checking.

Data inside the computer and printer is processed as parallel 8-bit words, so they must be disassembled for serial transmission, then reassembled after being received. The critical process of parallel-to-serial and serial-to-parallel conversion is handled by an integrated circuit called a *universal asynchronous receiver/transmitter* (or UART). This device is universal because it deals with ASCII codes. Asynchronous communication can take place at any time. Unlike the parallel interface, extra control lines are not always necessary to coordinate the flow of data. As a result, the UART never knows when a new character is going to arrive. Finally, a UART can either send or receive data.

Before a UART can send a data word, it must attach from two to four extra bits to the data stream, as shown in Fig. 2-18. When the transmit or receive data line is

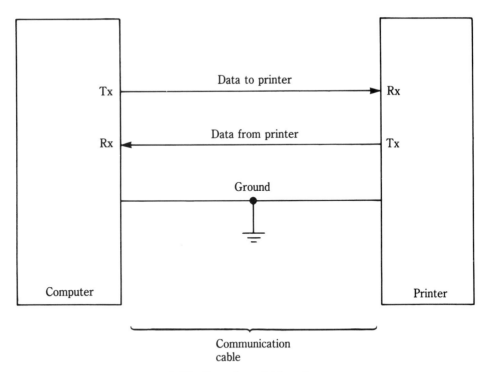

2-17 Generic serial interface.

idle, it rests at a binary 1 level. The UART inserts a single binary 0 as a *start bit* before the data stream. The first binary 0 is always considered to be the start bit. The next bits compose the actual ASCII or graphic code. There may be seven or eight bits depending on the particular convention that is selected. As a general rule, eight bits of data is typical, enabling the word to express codes from 0 to 255.

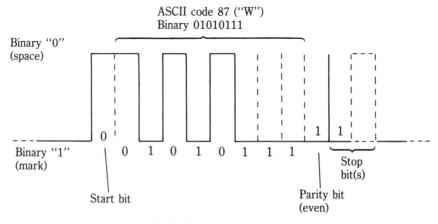

2-18 Serial data word.

Parity and stop bits also must be included. *Parity* is a simple method of checking serial data for errors. Even parity adds an extra bit to produce an even number of binary 1s in the data word. Odd parity adds an extra bit to produce an odd number of binary 1s in the data word. When a UART converts a parallel word into serial bits, it counts the number of 1s. If even parity is chosen and the number of 1s is odd, a binary 1 is inserted as the parity bit. If the number of 1s is already even, the parity bit is a binary 0. If odd parity is selected and the number of 1s is even, a binary 1 is generated as the parity bit. If the number of 1s is already odd, the parity bit is binary 0. A receiving UART also counts 1s in the data word and calculates its own parity bit, which it compares to the received parity bit. When the state of both parity bits match, data is assumed to be valid. If both parity bits do not match, the receiving UART flags an error and sends an error code to the computer. A parity bit is not mandatory for serial communication.

Finally, the data word must be ended. A UART adds one or two *stop bits* to the end of the data stream. Stop bits are always binary 1. After the selected number of stop bits is sent, the data line is returned to a binary 1 level and a new word can be sent.

A UART can be configured to work with a variety of parameters. It always adds one start bit. It might send seven or eight data bits. It might include an even or odd parity bit (or none at all). It adds one or two stop bits. Each selection can usually be set with a series of small switches (called *dip switches*) contained in the

UART disassembles a parallel word at the computer, and sends one bit at a time to the printer. A UART in the printer reassembles the original word.

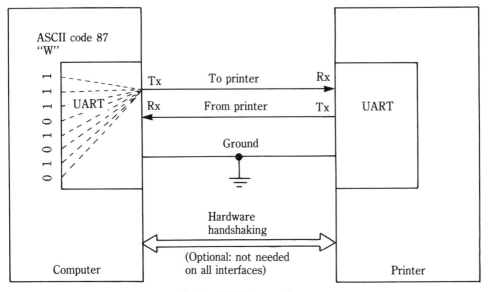

2-19 UART operation.

printer. Remember that both the computer and printer must have *exactly* the same settings. If not, serial data will be lost in a jumble of confusion.

Another important consideration is the speed at which bits are transferred. This is known as the *baud rate*. Baud rate is simply the rate at which serial data is transmitted, and is measured in bits per second (bps). For example, if a computer sends 1200 bps, the baud rate is 1200. Serial printers may offer rates as slow as 300 baud and as fast as 38,400 baud. Baud rate can also be selected in many cases using dip switches in the printer.

Figure 2-19 is a diagram for a typical serial communication link. Note that the transmit line from the printer is connected to the receive line of the printer, and vice versa. A ground wire serves as a common reference point between computer and printer circuits. Electrically speaking, these are the only three wires required to form a serial interface.

Serial handshaking can be provided through either software or hardware. Software handshaking takes advantage of the bidirectional nature of serial communication by allowing the printer to send serial codes back to the computer. These ASCII handshaking codes are known as *XON/XOFF* and *ETX/ACK*. They serve the same functions as "ready" and "busy" lines in a parallel interface. Older serial interfaces often use hardware handshaking instead of software control codes.

Hardware handshaking does not normally allow data transfer from printer to computer. Instead, an additional handshaking line signals the computer that the printer is busy. Some interfaces carry more than one handshaking line. Serial handshaking schemes vary somewhat between printer generations, so pay particular attention to the wiring in your serial printer's cable. Be sure that all signal lines are connected.

As you might imagine, serial interfaces can present a great deal of confusion. Many long hours of frustration and troubleshooting can be prevented by ensuring that printer cables are intact and dip switches have been set correctly. In spite of their added operating complexity, serial communication is extremely popular because of its bidirectional nature, flexibility, and ability to work well over long distances. Now that you understand the principles of printer communication, the next section of this chapter examines the actual applications of communication links.

Communication standards

There are literally hundreds of ways to implement parallel or serial interfaces. Many versions of both interfaces have been tried and abandoned since the early days of printers. The evolution of technology favors the best methods and techniques, so those that work well and can grow with advances in technology often develop into standards that other manufacturers adopt in the future. Standards are basically a detailed set of rules that clearly define the construction, connection, and operation of a circuit of system—in this case, a communication interface. By adopting standards, manufacturers can be sure that printer brand "X" will operate just fine with computer brand "Y."

There are two widely accepted printer communication standards. The *Centronics* standard is the most popular parallel interface. Centronics Corporation was one of the original printer manufacturers, so they were able to establish an early lead in the marketplace with their designs. The speed and reliability of the Centronics parallel interface soon made it an accepted standard in the industry. A serial approach emerged when the Electronics Industry Association (EIA) developed a comprehensive serial standard which they dubbed "Recommended Standard-232," or *RS-232* as we know it. The EIA designed RS-232 not just for printers, but as a universal interface for *any* serial device such as a modem, video monitor, or keyboard. As a generic standard, it offers a wide range of features and options, not all of which are necessary for printers, so it is rather lengthy and complex. Many manufacturers chose to use the signals and features that they thought were necessary. This fragmented the use of RS-232 so that not all devices were compatible with one another.

Over time, the EIA has updated and revised RS-232. The latest version of the serial standard is known as RS-232-D (for revision level D), although for this discussion it will simply be called RS-232. Most printer manufacturers have finally adopted a consistent use of the RS-232 standard, so there are very few instances of incompatible devices compared to the early use of RS-232.

Centronics

A Centronics interface connects a 25-pin subminiature D connector (Fig. 2-20) at the computer to a 36-pin Centronics connector at the printer. The size and shape of connectors used is part of the standard, so whenever you see a Centronics connector as shown in Fig. 2-21, you know that it supports a parallel interface. Since the Centronics connector has more pins than the 25-pin connector at the computer's parallel port, extra pins are not used. Each signal line will carry a conventional dig-

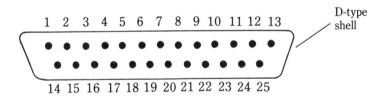

2-20   Standard connector—subminiature D-type, 25-pin.

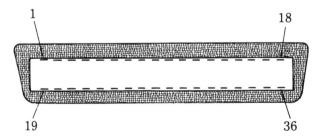

2-21   Standard connector—Centronics-type, 36-pin.

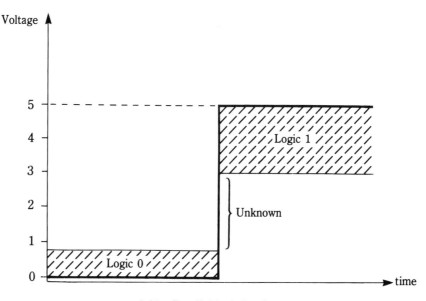

2-22 Parallel logic levels.

ital logic signal, so a binary 0 (or logic 0) will be about 0 volts, and a binary 1 (or logic 1) will be from 3 to 5 volts. These logic signals can be measured with a multimeter, which will be discussed in chapter 3. Figure 2-22 illustrates the relationship between voltage and logic levels.

Figure 2-23 demonstrates a typical interface between a computer and a parallel printer. When the printer is turned on, a binary 1 on the *select line* informs the computer that a printer is available. A binary 0 on the *busy line* and a short binary pulse on the *acknowledge line* requests data from the computer whenever it is ready. Figure 2-24 shows the signal pattern for this initialization.

Data bits are placed on *data lines* 1 through 8 by the computer. Ground lines 1 through 8 provide electrical reference points for each data bit. Note that not all versions of the Centronics interface use individual grounds for each data bit. Some versions only use one signal ground as a common reference point. After valid data is applied, a brief binary 0 pulse on the *data strobe* line latches data into the printer. Data is stored in a print buffer where it is processed and printed. A binary 1 busy signal from the printer causes the computer to wait before sending more data. When the printer is ready to accept new ASCII codes, its busy signal returns to a binary 0 level and it sends a brief binary 0 acknowledge pulse to request additional characters from the computer. Figure 2-25 shows the signals encountered in the interface.

Note the shaded areas for each data line. This means data can be either 1 or 0—it really does not affect the computer's actions. You may have noticed that some signal names have solid bars over them while others do not. These are called "active-low" logic signals. The acknowledge line is a prime example of this. You normally think that a signal is OFF (binary 0) and will be turned ON (binary 1) when a signal condition is true. This is known as "active-high" logic. In active-low

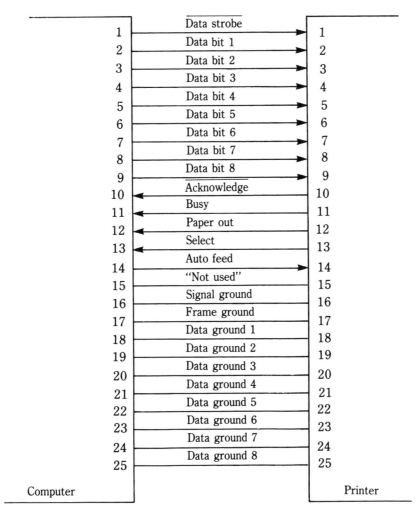

2-23 Centronics parallel interface.

logic, a signal is a binary 1 when it is OFF, and binary 0 when its signal condition is true. Both active-high and active-low logic signals can work together in the same system.

When the printer's paper supply is exhausted, a *paper out* error signal becomes binary 1 as shown in Fig. 2-26. As this happens, the select signal falls to a binary 0 and the busy signal remains at a binary 1 until paper is replaced and the printer's "On-Line" or "Select" key is pressed.

RS-232

Typical applications of RS-232 use subminiature D connectors like the one shown in Fig. 2-20 at both the printer and computer ends. However, since a serial data

*Signals during parallel printer power-up

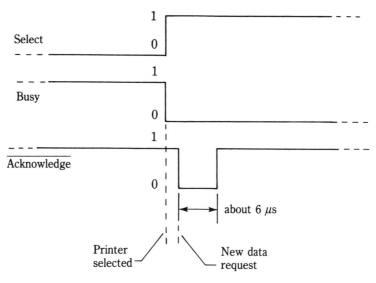

2-24 Initialization signal patterns.

link can be implemented with fewer than 6 wires, a 9-pin version of a subminiature D connector might be found at the computer's serial port.

Signal levels found in RS-232 are not represented by 0 volts and +5 volts as they are in the Centronics interface. They are somewhat more complicated. A logic 1 (or *mark* in RS-232) is represented by a −10 volt level. A logic 0 (called a *space*) is shown by a +10 volt level. Any hardware handshaking signals can be a logic 1 at +10 volts, or a logic 0 at −10 volts. Notice how the logical conventions are reversed between data and handshaking signals. The advantage of this dual-polarity (or *bi-polar*) logic is that it can be received accurately by circuits that are a great distance apart. Figure 2-27 shows the relationship of serial logic to voltage levels. It also shows how serial signal voltages compare to parallel signal voltages. These voltage levels can be read with a multimeter.

An RS-232 interface is shown in Fig. 2-28. As with the Centronics interface, there are ground wires to provide protection and signal reference between computer and printer. Data leaves the computer at the transmit data (Tx) pin and enters the printer at its receive data (Rx) pin. Data sent back from the printer leaves its own Tx pin and reaches the computer's Rx pin. When no data is being sent, data lines are held in the mark (−10 volt) condition. Remember that the first space (+10 volt) signal represents the start bit of a new serial word.

Serial handshaking can be accomplished through software or hardware. Software handshaking is handled by sending control characters from the printer to the computer. These control characters perform the same function as the busy line in a parallel interface. One control code (usually an ASCII XON or ETX) represents a

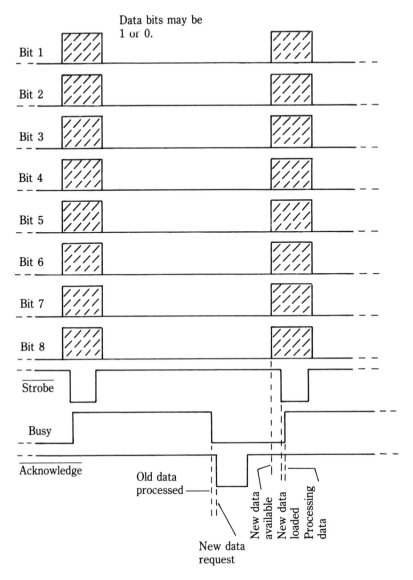

2-25   Data transfer signal patterns.

busy condition, while an opposing control code (normally XOFF or ACK) represents an acknowledge pulse meaning that the printer is ready for more information. In this way, all serial transfer can be handled with 3 wires; Tx, Rx, and ground.

Hardware handshaking uses an independent *data terminal ready* (DTR) Line to supply a busy signal to the computer's *data set ready* (DSR) pin. If hardware hand-

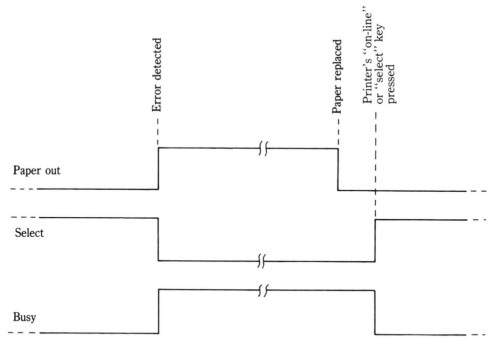

2-26 Error signal patterns.

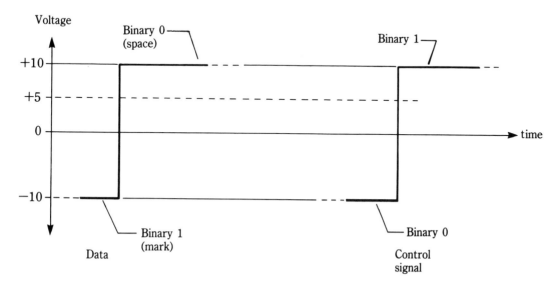

2-27 Serial logic levels.

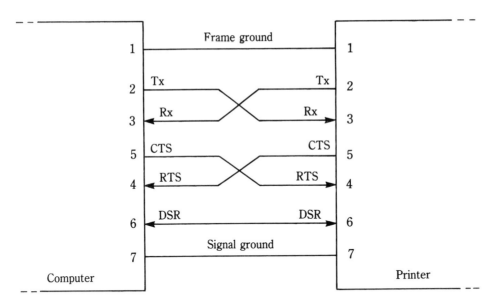

2-28 Typical RS232 interface.

shaking is used, no data is sent from the printer. Some printers support both methods of handshaking and can switch from one method to the other on demand.

Some older RS-232 interfaces can incorporate two additional signals. The *clear-to-send* (CTS) and *request-to-send* (RTS) signals are used most commonly in modem applications, but some printer interfaces might still require that these lines be connected to support another level of handshaking.

Chapter 3

Troubleshooting guidelines

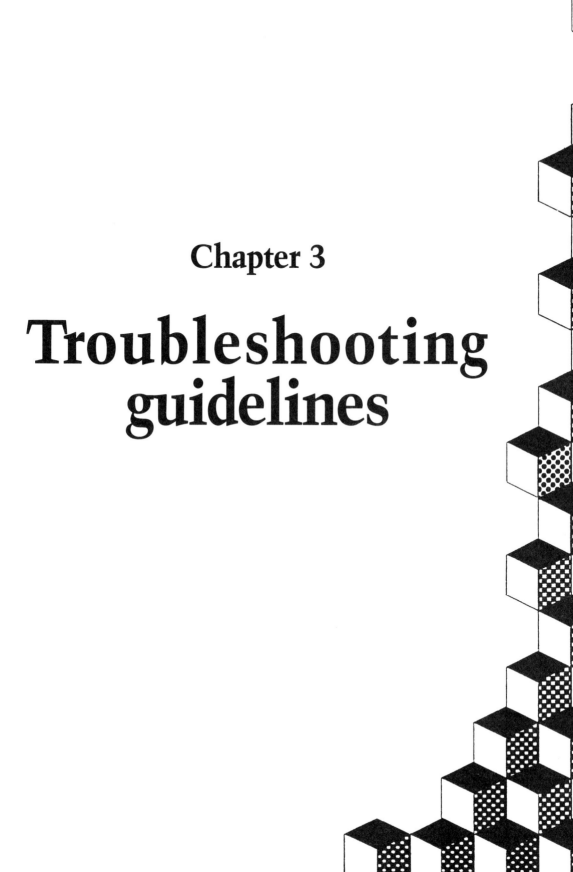

In the first two chapters, you learned some of the basics about printer technology. You learned what printers are, what their available technologies are, how to understand their specifications, and where some of their problem areas lie. You have also been introduced to major printer components and reviewed printer communications concepts and techniques in detail. Chapter 3 teaches you how to evaluate printer problems and gives you the solid approach needed to perform your own repairs.

Evaluating problems

There are four basic steps to all troubleshooting procedures as shown in Fig. 3-1: define the symptoms; identify and isolate the potential source (or location) of the problem; replace or repair the suspected subsection or component; and retest the system to be sure that you have solved the problem. If you have not solved the problem, start again from step one. This is a universal troubleshooting procedure that can be applied not only to printer repair, but to any type of repair.

Define the symptoms

Sooner or later, your printer is going to break down. It may be as simple as a sticky gear, or as complicated as an extensive electronic failure. Before you open up your toolbox, however, you must have a firm understanding of the symptoms. It is not enough to simply say "it's busted." Define your symptoms! Ask yourself what is happening (or better yet—what is *not* happening). When is it happening?

If this is a new installation, ask yourself if the computer is set up properly, or if the right cables are being used, or if configuration switches (or jumper wires) are set correctly. If you have used your printer for awhile, do you remember the last time you cleaned and lubricated it? Is the print light or missing? Is the print head moving freely? Ask yourself as many questions as possible. Understanding the symptoms makes it much easier to trace the problem to its appropriate subsection or components.

Use your senses to observe the printer and write down as many symptoms as you can. This may sound tedious now, but when the printer is disassembled and you are up to your elbows in repair work, a written record of symptoms and circumstances will keep you focused on the problems at hand instead of becoming lost in a maze of wires and components. This is even *more* important if you are a novice troubleshooter.

Identify and isolate the problem

Before you try to isolate a problem within the printer, you must first be sure that the printer itself is the source of the problem. In many cases, this is fairly obvious, but there are some situations that might be ambiguous (e.g., no printing with

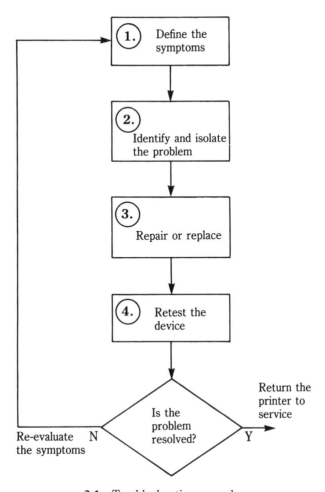

3-1 Troubleshooting procedure.

power on, erratic printing, missing characters, etc.). Remember that a printer is itself a subsection of a larger system made up of computer, printer, and an interconnecting cable. It is always possible that a computer failure, software error, or cable problem may be causing your symptoms.

You can easily apply the universal troubleshooting procedure here. After you have defined your symptoms, isolate the printer by removing it from its communication cable, then testing it on another computer with a working printer. A friend or colleague might let you test your printer on their computer system. If your printer exhibits the same symptoms on another system, there is an excellent probability that the problem is truly in the printer itself. You can then proceed with specific printer troubleshooting procedures. However, if those symptoms disappear and your printer works properly, you should suspect a problem at your computer or interconnecting cable. If you wish to confirm your observations, try a working printer on your computer system.

When you are confident that your printer is at fault, you can identify the suspected source of the problem. Start at the subsection level. You may recall from chapter 2 that there are typically five components within a printer: the paper feed assembly, the print head assembly, the carriage assembly, the power supply, and the electronic control package. Your printer's particular problem is probably rooted in at least one of these five components. The troubleshooting discussions in chapters 4, 5, 6, and 7 aid you in deciding which component is probably at fault. Only after you understand your symptoms and identify the possible problem should you ever attempt an actual repair.

Replace or repair

Now that you understand what is wrong and where to look, you can begin the actual repair procedures that should correct the problem(s). Some procedures require simple adjustments or cleaning, while others might require the exchange of electronic or mechanical parts, but all procedures are important and should be followed carefully.

Parts can generally be categorized as components or subsections. Component parts are the smallest possible individual parts that you can work with. Typical components are resistors, capacitors, gears, motors, integrated circuits, and belts. As a general rule, components cannot be repaired, only replaced. A subsection part (also called a subassembly) is composed of a variety of individual components. This means that a subsection can be repaired by locating and replacing any damaged components. For example, a broken carriage assembly might be repaired by locating and replacing an inoperative component such as a carriage motor. It is also possible to replace an entire subassembly, but they are often much more expensive and difficult to obtain.

Replacement components may be purchased from a variety of sources. You might try the manufacturer first, but not all manufacturers sell parts to the general public. Mail-order electronic stores such as those listed in appendix D can often provide general-purpose electronic components such as resistors, capacitors, diodes, transistors, integrated circuits, and motors. Some suppliers can provide more specialized parts for your printer such as belts, pulleys, and gears. Many of these companies are happy to send you their complete catalogs or product listings, so feel free to call.

If you reach a roadblock and must leave your repair for more than a day or two, be sure to reassemble your printer as much as possible before leaving it. This prevents a playful pet, curious child, or well-meaning spouse from accidentally misplacing or discarding parts while the printer sits on your workbench—you also will not forget how to put it back together later on.

Retest the printer

When your repair is finally complete and the printer is fully reassembled, it must be tested thoroughly before it is returned to service. Turn the printer on and run an internal *self test*. This shows the operation of the print head, carriage, paper advance, power supply, and much of the electronic control package. If you find that symptoms still persist, you will have to reevaluate them and start over. If normal operation is restored (or significantly improved), test the printer with a computer and return it to service.

Do not be discouraged if the printer still malfunctions. Simply walk away, clear your head, then start again by evaluating your symptoms. Never continue with a repair if you are tired or frustrated—tomorrow is another day. You should also realize that there might be more than one bad component to deal with. Remember that a printer is just a collection of assemblies, and each assembly is a collection of components. Normally, everything works together, but when one part fails, it can cause one or more adjacent parts to fail as well. You might have to make several attempts before the printer is completely repaired.

Disassembly and reassembly

You have to disassemble your printer in order to reach most subsections. While the actual process of disassembly is usually straightforward, there are some important points for you to keep in mind while you are working with the printer.

Disassembly

Most printer enclosures are designed in two halves as shown in Fig. 3-2. By removing the top cover, some or all major subsections should be exposed. However, removing the top cover is not always as easy as it might seem. Examine your enclosure very carefully. Some enclosures are held together with simple screws, just as they have been since printers first came out. Other enclosures use unusual screws such as Torx or Spline, or they incorporate cleverly hidden hooks or latches that

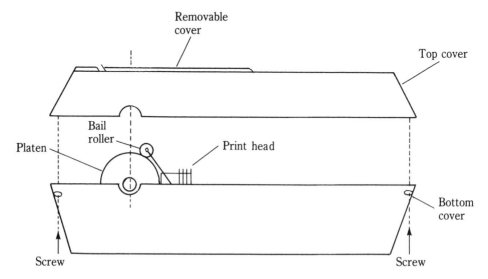

3-2 Typical printer housing assembly.

hold them together. Manufacturers complicate these enclosures intentionally to prevent unauthorized individuals from working on their printers, so be aware that you might need special tools, or the assistance of one or two other people to disassemble your printer without damaging the plastic enclosures.

Hazardous voltages

Printers use ac line voltages of 120 volts ac (220 volts ac in Europe). This is a hazardous and potentially *deadly* voltage level because under the right circumstances, it can supply enough current through your body to stop your heart. Since it only takes about 100 milliamps ($1/10$ of one ampere) of current flow to cause death, and a typical printer fuse may be rated for one or two amps, fuses and circuit breakers will not protect you.

Electrostatic printers generate extremely high voltage—easily in excess of 1000 volts dc. Although the small currents associated with these high voltages are far less likely to be fatal, a 1000 volt shock can still produce injury, burns, or unconsciousness. Many probe wires used with standard multimeters do not insulate voltages much more than 600 volts, so you can receive a shock right from your test probes. As a precaution, use high-voltage test probes when working with high-voltage power supplies, or troubleshoot "symptomatically"—that is, replace components based upon the symptoms of the printer instead of taking actual measurements.

Take the following five steps to protect yourself from injury:

1. Keep the printer unplugged (not just turned off) as much as possible during disassembly and repair. Some service procedures will require that the printer be powered, so plug in just long enough to perform your tests, then unplug the printer again.

2. If you must work with the power supply, try to wear rubber gloves. This will insulate your hands and forearms just like insulation on a wire. You might think that rubber gloves are inconvenient and uncomfortable, but they are far better than the inconvenience and discomfort of an electric shock. Also wear a long-sleeve shirt or sweater with the sleeves rolled down.

3. If rubber gloves are absolutely out of the question, remove all metal jewelry and work with one hand behind your back. Gold, silver, and stainless steel in your jewelry are excellent conductors. Should your wedding ring or watch strap hook onto a live ac wire, it will conduct current directly to your skin. By keeping one hand behind your back, you cannot grasp both ends of a live ac line and cause a path of current through your heart.

4. Be sure to use high-voltage probes when checking high-voltage power supplies. Remember that standard commercial probe leads do not necessarily have the *dielectric strength* (or insulating properties) to protect you from a shock.

5. Treat electricity with respect. Whenever electronic circuitry is exposed (especially power supply circuitry), a shock hazard does exist. Keep in mind

that it is the flow of current, not the voltage potential, that can injure you. Insulate yourself as well as possible from any exposed wiring.

Keep notes of your work

You might think that notes are a waste of time, but a few well-drawn diagrams and carefully written observations can clear up a great deal of confusion and uncertainty when you must reassemble the printer again. Certainly, it is not necessary to record each individual step that you take during the repair, but you should denote important things. For example, if you are disassembling the printer, show the orientation and order of mechanical parts such as levers, gears, or springs. Notes are especially important if you must leave during your repair. They remind you where each part goes, and what you have already accomplished.

Reassembly

There is a popular myth among consumers that manufacturers use extra parts in a product just to make it more complicated. Each new generation of products is certainly more sophisticated than the last, but there is no such thing as a "useless" part where consumer electronics is concerned. Printer manufacturers simply cannot afford to waste money or labor assembling parts that serve no purpose. Competition is so intense that manufacturers actually try to make their products as simple as possible. As a result, it is important that you keep track of every part that you remove from your printer and that every part is replaced correctly during reassembly. If you have parts left over, then you have overlooked something important. Recheck your assembly and make sure that all parts are placed properly. Do *not* attempt to operate your printer unless all parts are replaced correctly!

Electrical repairs

Many of the troubleshooting procedures in this book involve the printer's power supply and electronic circuitry. Those procedures guide you in isolating and replacing suspect components, but before you begin a repair, you should be familiar with the variety of components that you will encounter and what they do. You should also be able to recognize six general types of components on sight; resistors, capacitors, transformers (inductors), diodes, transistors, and integrated circuits (ICs).

Resistors

Simply stated, a *resistor* inhibits the flow of current—that's all it does! It can be used to adjust and control levels of current and voltage at various points in a circuit. As a result, resistance is a valuable and vital factor in electronics. A cross-section of a typical resistor is shown in Fig. 3-3. It works because carbon filling is not as good of a conductor as metal. Therefore, it wastes some energy when current flows through the carbon, offering resistance. Carbon filling can be formulated to provide just about any value of resistance. Appendix C shows a standard

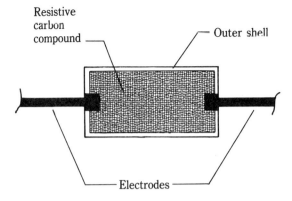

3-3   Cross-sectional view of a typical resistor.

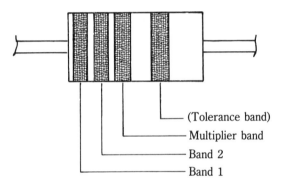

3-4   Basic resistor type—carbon composition resistor.

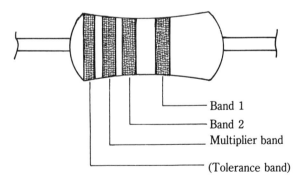

3-5   Basic resistor type—carbon film resistor.

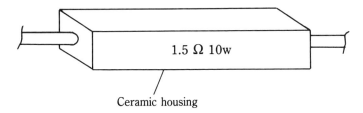

1.5 Ω 10w

Ceramic housing

3-6 Basic resistor type—ceramic (power) resistor.

color code chart for reading resistors. The measure of resistance is the *ohm*, which is represented by the Greek letter omega (Ω).

There are three basic types of resistor as shown in Figs. 3-4 through 3-6: carbon composition, carbon film, and ceramic. The differences between them are only in their construction and materials, but each type is read the same way using the standard color codes. You might often find that ceramic resistors (typically used for large, high-power resistors) have their resistance value printed in numbers on their surfaces.

Reading a color code is not as hard as it might look at first glance. Color bands are read from left to right starting from the band that is closest to the resistor's edge. A resistor's value is indicated by the first three colors—two value bands times a multiplier band. For example, suppose the first three color bands are green, red, and brown. The value of the resistor is then the first two colors (green = 5, red = 2, or 52) multiplied by the power of the third band (brown = × 10). That resistor is then 52 × 10, or 520 ohms. You can confirm this by measuring the resistor with a multimeter. If you see a color pattern of red, violet, and orange, the resistor would be (red = 2, violet = 7, orange = × 10,000) 27,000 ohms. Another way of stating this would be 27 kilo-ohms. The term *kilo* means thousand. Resistors over one million ohms are expressed in mega-ohms. The term *mega* means million.

You might see a fourth band on the resistor. This is a tolerance band indicating how much the resistor may be off from its marked value. A gold band indicates a tolerance of ± 5%, a silver band indicates a tolerance of ± 10% and no band tells you that tolerance is ± 20%. For most purposes, you will be using 5% or 10% resistors.

Capacitors

Capacitance, like resistance, is a vital property in electronics, and capacitors are widely used as filters and timing components. The purpose of a capacitor is to hold an electric charge. This ability is a simple process, but it has powerful applications. You will learn about the power filtering action of capacitors in chapter 5. The value of a capacitor is measured in *farads* (F). The more farads a capacitor is built for, the more electrical charge it holds, and vice versa. In reality, one farad is a tremendous amount of capacitance. Most capacitors are built in the micro-farad (μF, or millionths of a farad) range. Even smaller capacitors exist in the pico-farad (pF, or 10^{-12} farad) range.

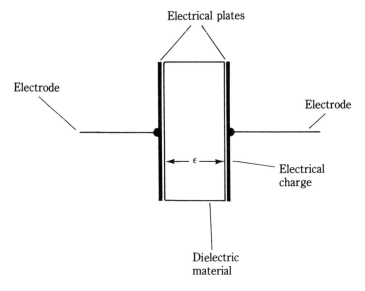

3-7 Cross-sectional view of a generic capacitor.

The cross-section of a generic capacitor is shown in Fig. 3-7. Two conductive plates are separated by a dielectric (insulating) material. When a voltage is applied across the capacitor, an electrical charge is built up between the plates. When voltage is removed, plates tend to retain the charge. Use caution when working with charged capacitors. Larger capacitors can store enough charge to be dangerous.

There are five common types of capacitor: paper, mica, ceramic, tantalum, and electrolytic. Figure 3-8 shows some of these devices. Capacitors can be catego-

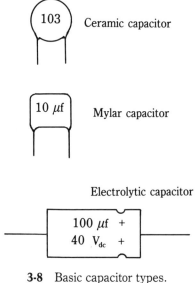

3-8 Basic capacitor types.

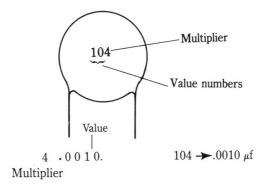

3-9 Ceramic capacitor markings.

rized as *polarized* or *nonpolarized*. A polarized capacitor has a set anode and cathode defined by its internal construction, so it must be inserted into a circuit in the proper orientation. If it is not inserted correctly, it will malfunction. In extreme cases, the reversed capacitor can even explode. Nonpolarized capacitors have no particular polarity, so they can be used in any orientation. As a general rule, always check a capacitor for polarity markings.

Capacitors do not use a color coding system like resistors do. Values of capacitance are written directly onto the part in plain English, or as a numeric code as shown in Fig. 3-9. A numeric code usually consists of 3 digits. The first two digits indicate the general value of the part, while the third digit tells how many places to move the decimal place to the *left*. In the example in Fig. 3-9, the part marked "104" indicates a magnitude of 10, with the decimal place moved four places to the left (0.001). This is read as 0.001 μF (microfarads). You can confirm this value by measuring the part with a capacitance checker. Your multimeter might have a built-in capacitance checker. The number 103 is read as 0.01 μF, and so on.

Inductors

Inductors use current in a circuit to establish a magnetic field that is proportional to the current flow in the inductor. Advances in solid-state electronics have rendered inductors essentially obsolete in traditional applications such as resonant (tuned) circuits and oscillators, but they remain very valuable components in such

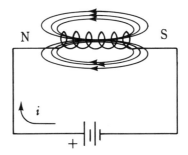

3-10 A generic inductor.

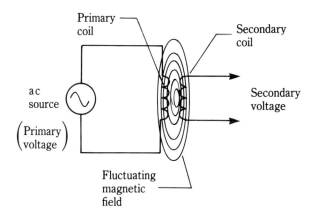

3-11   A basic transformer.

printer parts as power transformers, motors, and solenoids. A basic inductor is shown in Fig. 3-10.

As ac flows through the coil, a varying magnetic field is produced. If a secondary coil is placed nearby, as in Fig. 3-11, the force of the magnetic field intersecting the secondary coil induces a secondary ac voltage on the secondary coil's output. This type of *magnetic coupling* only works when current in the primary coil is changing constantly, and is the basic principle behind all transformers. Transformers are discussed in chapter 5.

If a *permeable* material (a material which can be magnetized) such as cobalt, iron, or steel is placed within the influence of the inductor's magnetic field, force is exerted on the material and it is pulled toward the magnetic field as shown in Fig. 3-12. The ability to move solid objects with magnetic force is the basis for motors and solenoids, discussed in chapter 7.

Inductance is measured in *henries* (H); however, this is rarely an important specification in transformers, motors or solenoids. For the purposes of this book, you will not be concerned with the inductance value of these parts.

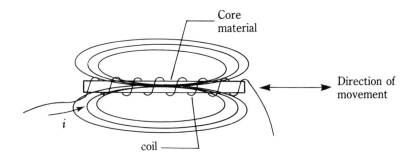

3-12   A basic solenoid.

Diodes

Diodes are two-terminal semiconductor devices that permit current to flow in one direction *only*, and prohibit current flow in the other direction. This process, known as *rectification*, is critical to the successful operation of power supplies and many other circuits. Figure 3-13 is a diagram of a typical diode. Its schematic symbol and forward current direction are shown in Fig. 3-14. As you might expect, a

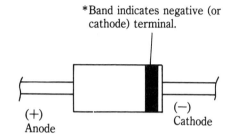

3-13   Semiconductor diode—part drawing.

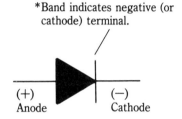

3-14   Semiconductor diode—schematic symbol.

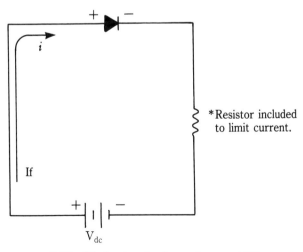

3-15   Diode circuit—forward current (If).

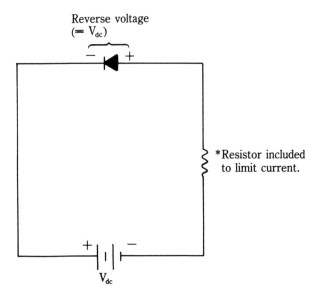

Reverse voltage
($= V_{dc}$)

*Resistor included
to limit current.

V_{dc}

3-16   Diode circuit—reverse voltage.

diode is a polarized device, so it must be inserted in its proper orientation with respect to the circuit's polarity.

When discussing diodes, you should pay attention to two key specifications: *forward current* rating (I_f), and *peak inverse voltage* rating (PIV). Forward current is the maximum current that can flow through a diode before damage occurs. Figure 3-15 shows a forward-biased diode. When the current flowing through the diode exceeds I_f, the diode fails. When a diode is biased in the reversed direction as in Fig. 3-16, no current flows unless the potential exceeds the value of PIV. Above this level, the diode breaks down and begins to conduct current. Note that diode part numbers start with a *1N* prefix (e.g., 1Nxxxx).

While exceeding a PIV rating destroys most rectifier-type diodes, some diodes are actually designed to operate in this breakdown region. These are known as *zener* diodes. Although zener and rectifier diodes look roughly identical, the zener's operation allows it to function as a voltage regulator in some power supply circuits.

Transistors

A transistor is a three-terminal semiconductor device designed to provide signal amplification or switching functions in a circuit. The same transistor can amplify *or* switch depending on how its surrounding circuit supplies *bias* (idle voltage with no signal present). Transistors are available in many shapes and sizes to meet various space and power-dissipation requirements. As a rule of thumb, you can assume that larger transistor packages are built to dissipate larger amounts of power. Figures 3-17 through 3-19 illustrate several common package styles. The TO-3 case in Fig. 3-19 has only two pins. Its metal case is the third pin.

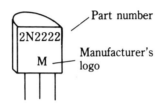

3-17 Transistor package—TO-92.

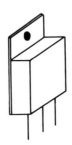

3-18 Transistor package—TO-220

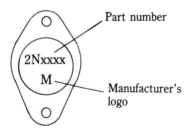

3-19 Transistor package—TO-3.

Transistors can be manufactured as *bipolar* or *field effect* devices. Bipolar devices may be either npn or pnp, while a field-effect transistor (FET) may be described as N-channel or P-channel. These differences involve the basic materials and fabrication techniques used to manufacture transistors, so it is impossible to tell whether a device is bipolar or field effect simply by its case style. Although their operating principles and bias needs are different, both types of transistors may amplify or switch. Transistor part numbers start with a *2N* prefix (e.g., 2Nxxxx). You can learn about the characteristics and performance of any transistor by looking up its part number in a manufacturer's data book. Data books can be obtained through some vendors listed in appendix D.

As you might have guessed, all transistors are polarized devices. Bipolar leads are called Emitter, Base, and Collector, while FET leads are called Source, Gate, and Drain. Manufacturer's data books, as well as many replacement part packages, name each lead—they are rarely marked on the part itself. If you are in doubt, make notes of how the original parts are installed! When you must replace a faulty transistor, you might be able to find a suitable replacement part from a source other than the original manufacturer by using any cross-reference indices included in a data book. This lists its generic part number (2Nxxxx) and the equivalent part numbers offered by one or more manufacturers. Under most circumstances, an "equivalent" part made by a different manufacturer will work fine, but all specifications might not match exactly.

Integrated circuits

Integrated circuits (ICs) are the most diverse and powerful group of components that you will ever deal with. They are the "building blocks" of modern electronic circuitry, and can provide incredibly complex analog and digital functions. ICs can be used as amplifiers, memories, digital logic, oscillators, regulators, or micropro-

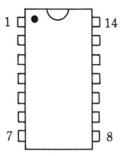

3-20 IC package—dual in-line package (DIP) style.

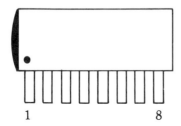

3-21 IC package—single in-line package (SIP) style.

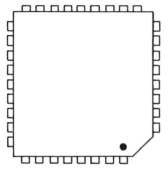

3-22 IC package—PLCC style.

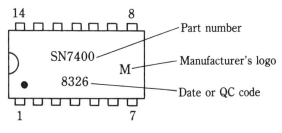

3-23   IC markings.

cessors, to name just a few. Figures 3-20 through 3-22 show several IC packages that you might encounter.

ICs are generally found in the dual in-line package (DIP) configuration, but the trend is moving rapidly toward surface-mounted components. DIP pins are numbered in a counter-clockwise fashion from a starting mark such as a circle or notch imprinted onto the housing, as shown in Fig. 3-23. Pin 1 is adjacent to the starting mark. While ICs are not polarized in the same sense as diodes or transistors, each IC pin does a specific job, so it is very important that you insert a new IC in the same orientation as the one you are removing, or the new IC will probably be destroyed. Refer to the manufacturer's data for a particular IC to learn what each pin does. If you have a schematic diagram for your printer, you might be able to estimate an IC's functions by the way it is interconnected with other components.

It is impossible to tell what an IC does or how it works simply by looking at it. You have to look up the part number from manufacturer's data based on the IC's part number. A part number code generally consists of a prefix that identifies the manufacturer, the part number itself, and a suffix which denotes a particular IC version or package type. By reviewing manufacturer's data, you can learn its specifications and operating conditions. Do not confuse the part number with any other date or quality control code that may also be printed on the part. Be aware that only one code is the actual part number.

Now that you have become familiar with a variety of electronic components, you can identify and read many of the components found in a printer's circuits. This is a great help in dealing with the electronic repairs in chapter 5 and 6.

Mechanical repairs

Repairing electronics is difficult because it defies the senses. You cannot "see" a circuit at work, only the end results of its operations. This is why test instruments such as multimeters and logic probes are needed—to expose the silent, invisible, lightning-fast signals that electronic circuits deal with. By comparison, mechanical repairs are much simpler. You can see and hear such things as sticky gears, loose belts, or jammed rollers.

Observe the problem

For mechanical repairs, a keen sense of sight, touch, and hearing are your best tools. These often lead you directly to the problem area. Closer observation might reveal a broken spring, metal shards, stripped gears, or other mechanical ailments.

Assembly and lubrication

Use common sense when adjusting and assembling mechanical parts. Avoid using excessive force on screws and bolts. This causes other parts to wear and jam. On the other hand, do not leave parts too loose. Vibrations shake apart loose components which can interfere with other parts and cause a problem even greater than the one you are trying to fix.

Go easy on the lubrication. A light, general-purpose household oil is often acceptable, but use it sparingly, and only in a few key places. Absolutely avoid using a heavy-duty lubricant such as motor oil or heavy grease. It might seem to be a good idea, but it will simply attract dirt and dust, which increase wear and tear in the very parts you wish to protect. It also makes future cleaning difficult and messy. Chapter 7 discusses mechanical repairs in more detail.

Using a test meter

Test meters have gone by many names. Some people call them *multimeters* or just *meters*, while others refer to them as voltohm milliammeters (VOM) or "multi-testers." For the purposes of this book, a *multimeter* is a test instrument capable of measuring several important electrical qualities such as voltage, current, and resistance. Regardless of what you call them, multimeters are the most handy and versatile tool that you will ever use when troubleshooting a printer's circuitry.

Multimeters are widely available through retail electronics stores. Perhaps the most accessible is your local Radio Shack store, but mail-order outlets such as those listed in appendix D might provide superior selections at comparable prices. A good-quality digital multimeter with such features as a continuity buzzer, capacitor checker, transistor checker, and diode checker can be purchased for under $100. The price is well worth its versatility and long life. As a standard, this book refers to a digital multimeter, but you might use just about any analog equivalent.

Chapter 1 introduced you briefly to analog and digital multimeters, as well as some of their measurement capabilities. In this section, you can see how to use a typical multimeter to read voltage, current, resistors, capacitors, diodes, and transistors.

Measuring voltage

A typical multimeter can measure dc voltages or ac voltages on several different scales ranging from millivolts to about 1000 volts. The important thing to remember is that all voltages (ac or dc) are measured *in parallel* with the desired component or source. Simply place your test leads *across* the part you are testing, as shown in Figs. 3-24 through 3-26. *Never* interrupt a circuit and attempt to measure voltage in series with other components. Any reading will be meaningless, and the circuit probably will not function.

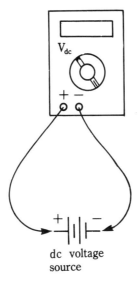

dc voltage
source

3-24 Measuring voltage—testing a battery or dc voltage source.

Suppose you wish to measure the dc voltage across a standard 1.5 volt dry cell battery as shown in Fig. 3-24. Set your multimeter to the next highest scale above 1.5 volts in the dc volts mode (a 2-volt scale is typical), then touch the meter's test leads to the positive (+) and negative (–) sides of the battery. You can then read the battery voltage directly from the meter's readout. If you connect the test leads

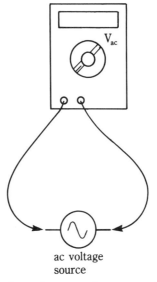

ac voltage
source

3-25 Measuring voltage—testing an ac voltage source.

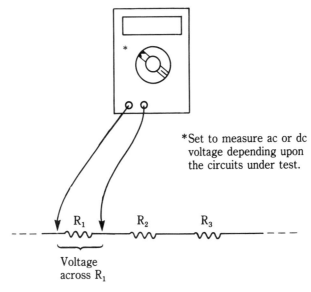

*Set to measure ac or dc
voltage depending upon
the circuits under test.

3-26 Measuring voltage across a component.

backwards on a digital meter, the display simply shows a negative number of the
same amount (try it). However, if test leads are reversed on an analog multimeter,
the needle cannot show a negative reading, so it buries itself below the zero line.
This might damage an analog meter movement.

Reading ac voltage is just as simple. In order to measure the ac voltage in your
wall outlet as in Fig. 3-25, set the multimeter to measure the next highest ac scale

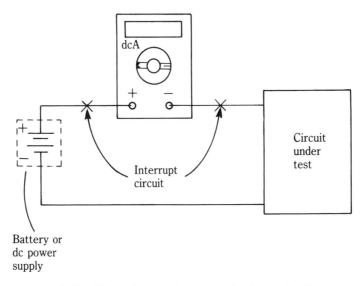

3-27 Measuring supply current feeding a circuit.

over 120 volts (a 200-volt scale is common). If you are attempting this in Europe, you would set it to the next scale above 220 volts (you might find a 750- or 1000-volt scale). Insert your test leads into the outlet prongs and read ac voltage directly from the meter.

CAUTION: ac line voltages can be extremely hazardous! Be sure that you are properly insulated at *all times*!

Test lead polarity is not important when measuring ac voltages. Try reversing your leads—you will see the same reading. When working with an analog multimeter, be sure that its scale is set higher than the voltage to be measured. Otherwise, the needle "pegs out" or buries itself over the maximum end of the scale. This can also damage the analog meter movement. Digital multimeters are protected from damage when the test voltage exceeds its range. The digital display simply shows an "over-range" condition. Remember that ac voltages are measure in root mean square (rms).

Measuring ac or dc voltages across a component uses exactly the same principles as those described previously. Set your multimeter to the appropriate voltage scale in ac or dc mode. If you do not know what voltage to expect, it is always wise to set the scale to its maximum value to start. After you get an idea of the actual voltage level, you can reduce the voltage scale to read with greater precision.

Measuring current

Most general-purpose multimeters allow you to measure dc or ac current in a circuit, although there are usually not as many current ranges to choose from. Current is always measured *in series* with the particular circuit you are testing, as illustrated in Fig. 3-28. Placing your multimeter in series, however, is not always a simple task. In most cases, you must physically interrupt the circuit at the point you wish to measure, then insert the test leads across the break. It is easy to break into a circuit, but realize that you must also put the circuit back together when you are finished. Use your best judgment in choosing a place to measure current.

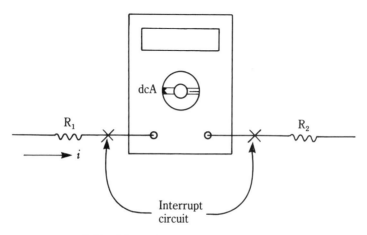

3-28 Measuring current within a circuit.

Never try to read current in parallel across a component. Under some conditions this might cause an inrush of current to the multimeter. If the current functions are not fused internally to protect its circuitry against such a surge, your multimeter will suffer permanent damage. Pay attention when measuring current.

To measure current in a circuit as in Fig. 3-27, it is necessary to break the circuit at any convenient point and insert the multimeter as shown. A sound practice is to turn off all power *before* interrupting the circuit, then insert the meter as required, and select the appropriate ac or dc current range. If you are not sure of the range, start with the maximum range setting. Then turn power back on. This procedure is especially important when measuring current within a circuit as in Fig. 3-28. Breaking a small portion of the circuit while power is on can cause the circuit to behave erratically or even cause a failure.

If you are using an analog meter, be sure that the meter's polarity and test range is correct with respect to the circuit under test. Otherwise, the needle tends to bury itself at either extreme stop when power is finally applied.

Checking a resistor

Resistance measurements are also handled by most commercial multimeters. Unlike voltage and current measurements, resistance tests are *static tests*—tests made with circuit power off. Resistance tests are made *in parallel* with the resistance to be measured. Select an appropriate range of resistance, then place your test leads across the resistance to be measured as shown in Fig. 3-29. There are often plenty of resistance ranges to choose from.

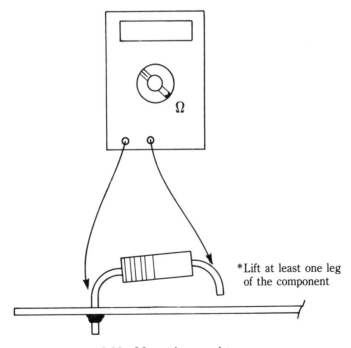

3-29   Measuring a resistor.

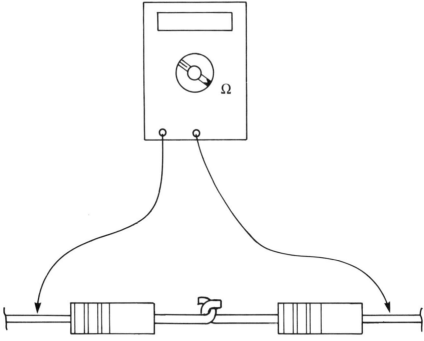

3-30 Measuring several resistors.

It is a good practice to isolate the part to be tested by removing at least one of its two leads from the circuit, as in Fig. 3-29. This prevents other components in the circuit from interacting with the desired resistance, which could produce an inaccurate reading. You can isolate a component by cutting one of its leads, or desoldering a lead from the printed circuit board. Desoldering takes longer, but it is the preferred technique.

The combined resistance of multiple components can be measured as shown in Fig. 3-30. Resistors might be connected in series, parallel, or any combination. Note that only resistors are shown here for the sake of simplicity, but there might be many different components configured together into a complex network. As long as power is not activated, your reading should be accurate to within the tolerance of the meter.

When measuring a discrete (individual) resistor, your reading should always fall within the tolerance rating of the resistor being measured. For example, a 1.0 kΩ resistor with a tolerance of 5% should read between 950 and 1050 ohms (0.950 to 1.05 kΩ). If that same resistor has a tolerance of 20%, you should measure anywhere from 800 to 1200 ohms (0.800 to 1.20 kΩ). Resistors are notoriously reliable components, so they do not wander from their rated values unless they are defective. Be sure to measure any resistors that appear discolored or burned.

Checking a capacitor

Not all multimeters are capable of directly measuring capacitance, but this can be a handy feature when you need it. Even if your multimeter does not have a built-in

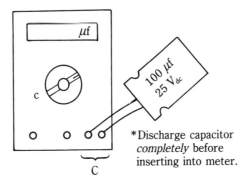

3-31 Checking a capacitor using a built-in capacitor checker.

capacitance checker, you still can make indirect checks of suspect capacitors using your meter's resistance function. As with resistance checks, all capacitance tests are *static* and *parallel*. The capacitor should have at least one lead removed from its circuit, and all circuit power should be off. A capacitor might have to be removed from its circuit entirely before it can be inserted into a capacitor checker as in Fig. 3-31.

Remember that a capacitor holds an electric charge. You must discharge the capacitor completely before inserting it into a checker like the one shown in Fig.

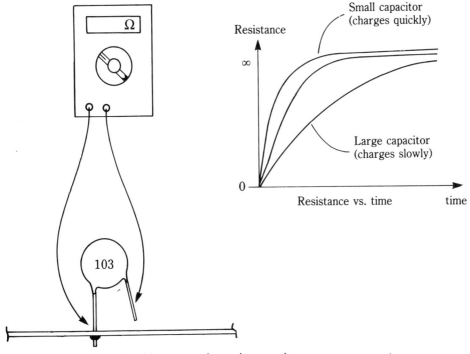

3-32 Checking a capacitor using a resistance measurement.

3-31. Any substantial charge could throw off the reading, or even damage the meter. Select a range of capacitance that is larger than the part under test, insert the part, and read its capacitance value (in microfarads) directly from the display. Capacitor tolerance is typically 20 percent unless it is marked otherwise, so a 1.0 μF capacitor might read between 0.8 μF and 1.2 μF. This kind of tolerance in a capacitor rarely affects a circuit's operation.

If you are using an analog meter, or your digital meter does not provide a capacitor-checker, you can use resistance to make "quick-and-dirty" judgments about suspect capacitors. Fig. 3-32 shows how to make the measurement. The principle behind this is simple: any ohmmeter provides a current source to the part being tested (this is why power in the circuit must be turned off). By connecting a discharged capacitor to an ohmmeter, you are essentially charging it. A capacitor charges quickly when first connected, resulting in a low resistance reading. Its rate of charging slows as it obtains a charge (the resistance measurement increases more and more slowly). When the capacitor is fully charged, the ohmmeter reads infinity. If the capacitor under test behaves this way, it is probably good.

You are not actually measuring resistance or capacitance here, but how the capacitor charges. If the capacitor is an open circuit, it will not take any charge at all, so you will only read infinity. If the capacitor is short-circuited, it will not accumulate a charge, so you will read only 0 ohms, or it might charge to some level below infinity and hang there. In either case, the capacitor is probably defective. If you are in doubt, check several other capacitors of the same value and compare their reactions to those of your suspect part.

Checking a diode

Diodes are surprisingly simple devices to check, but your multimeter must have a *diode-check* selection, or a *high-ohms* resistance scale. This is because most typical ohmmeter circuits use internal voltages that are too low to activate a diode (remember that ohmmeters supply their own power to check resistance). To measure diode resistance, your meter must have at least one scale that will supply enough voltage to successfully forward-bias (turn on) the diode.

Figure 3-33 illustrates the procedure for performing a *static* resistance check on a rectifier or small-signal diode. At least one lead of the part under test must be disconnected from the circuit and all power should be off. Set the multimeter range to measure diodes, then connect your test leads to forward-bias the diode as shown in Fig. 3-33. When a good diode is properly forward-biased, its resistance should be from 200 to 700 ohms. Small-signal diodes usually measure low (about 200 ohms), while rectifier diodes read higher (about 600 ohms). Reverse your test leads as shown in Fig. 3-34. This reverse-biases the diode. As a result, the diode does not turn on, and you should read infinite resistance.

If the diode is open-circuited, it will read infinite resistance in both directions. A short-circuited diode will read 0 ohms (or some very low resistance) in the forward direction, or in both directions. In either case, the diode is probably defective. You should replace it with a diode of equal I_f and PIV ratings.

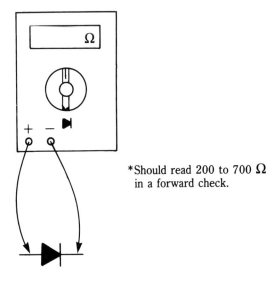

*Should read 200 to 700 Ω
in a forward check.

3-33   Checking a diode—forward bias check.

Checking a transistor

Bipolar transistors can be measured with either a transistor-checker built into your multimeter, or a variation of the static resistance check just discussed for diodes. To ensure an accurate reading using both techniques, the transistor under test must be removed entirely from its circuit.

Transistor checkers, such as those found on some digital multimeters, are used to evaluate *gain* (or *hfe*). Gain indicates the amount at which the base current is

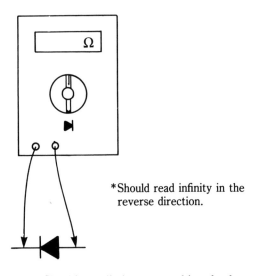

*Should read infinity in the
reverse direction.

3-34   Checking a diode—reverse-bias check.

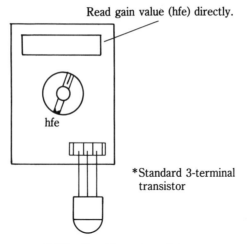

Read gain value (hfe) directly.

hfe

*Standard 3-terminal
transistor

3-35 Checking a transistor.

multiplied to form current in the collector (remember that bipolar transistors have three leads; the emitter, base, and collector). Figure 3-35 shows a basic multimeter transistor-checker. Set the multimeter to a gain or hfe range, then insert the transistor into its socket. Gain should read directly on the display. Be sure to insert the transistor in its proper orientation. Manufacturer's data will tell you which leads are the emitter, base, and collector, as well as how much gain to expect. If gain reads very low (or zero), the transistor might be internally shorted. A very high reading (or infinity) will suggest an open transistor. Replace any transistor with suspicious readings.

You can also check a transistor like a pair of back-to-back diodes as shown in Figs. 3-36 and 3-37. Although the structure and operation of transistors are somewhat more complex than this, you can perform static diode resistance checks on the *collector-base* and *emitter-base* junctions of npn and pnp transistors. First, check your collector-base junction just as you would check a rectifier diode. In the forward-bias direction, you should read 400 to 600 ohms. In the reverse-bias direction, you should read infinity. Repeat this check for the emitter-base junction.

Collector

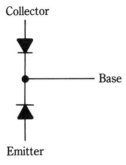

Base

Emitter

3-36 Transistor-diode relationship—PNP transistor.

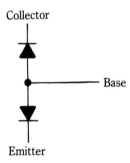

3-37 Transistor-diode relationship—NPN transistor.

Treat it just as if it were a diode. You should read resistance one way and infinity the other way. Finally, check your transistor in both directions from collector to emitter. It should read infinity in *both* directions. Note that the polarity of these "diode checks" is reversed from npn to pnp devices.

If either the collector-base or emitter-base junction appears open or shorted in both directions, the transistor is probably defective. A short-circuit reading from collector to emitter in either direction also indicates a damaged component. Replace any transistor that is suspect.

Chapter 4

Print head mechanisms

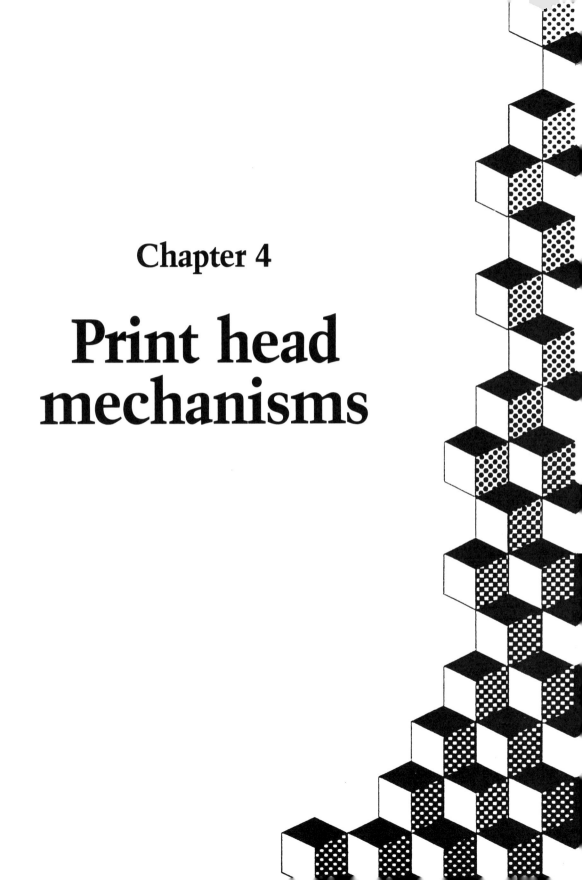

Print heads are used to deliver processed images to a page surface. The image might be a fully-formed character (in the case of a character printer), or a sequence of dots that are assembled to produce characters and graphic images. Print heads use four basic technologies to deliver images: impact, thermal, ink-jet, and electrostatic. These technologies are the foundation of modern computer printers. The remainder of the printer is designed—both electrically and mechanically—to accommodate the particular print head. In this chapter, you learn about the construction, operation, and repair of each type of print head.

Impact

Impact printer technologies fall into one of two categories: *character* or *dot matrix*. Dot matrix is by far the most widespread and popular technology, but this section briefly covers character printers as well.

Character printers

A character impact print head requires four key components as shown in Fig. 4-1: a print wheel, a print solenoid (known as a *hammer*), a motor, and a position encoder. As you learned in chapter 1, the print wheel (or die) contains reverse-molded letters, numbers, or special characters that are printed. The die mounts

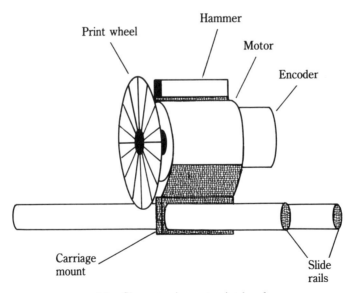

4-1   Character impact print head.

directly on a motor that rotates precisely to position each character. It is controlled by the printer's electronic control package. An encoder is attached to the motor. It rotates along with the motor and generates data codes that reveal the current orientation of the print wheel.

Using this technique, printer circuitry advances the motor and die to a desired letter position (the letter P, for example). When the motor has finished advancing, the circuitry reads the encoder's position. If this code matches the code executed by the printer, then the control circuitry knows that the motor has rotated correctly and the proper die (the letter P) is in place. Finally, a high-energy electrical pulse is sent to the hammer solenoid. The hammer rams the selected die against an inked ribbon and leaves a permanent image on the page.

After the hammer and die withdraw from the page, a carriage motor advances the assembly to a new character position, and the entire process is repeated.

Troubleshooting character print heads

Symptom Printing quality has become poor. Printed characters appear broken, tilted, missing, or otherwise distorted.

These symptoms are illustrated in Fig. 4-2. Every time a die strikes paper, it liberates a small amount of dust from the page surface. When this dust combines with the ribbon ink, it forms a kind of "glue" that can cake in and around molded characters. Over time, this glue hardens and causes a distorted, dirty appearance. Follow Procedure 4-1 when checking and cleaning a print wheel.

Other troubles usually indicate a ruined print wheel. Impact forces caused by a hammer's continuous pounding can eventually cause raised portions of a letter to break away, leaving obvious gaps in the die. Hammer forces can also cause a petal to bend out of alignment resulting in a tilted appearance. Excessive or sudden bending can wrench a petal off entirely. In any of these cases, the print wheel is ruined and will have to be replaced.

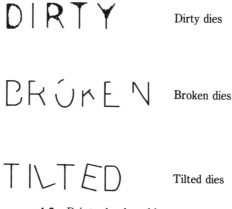

4-2 Print wheel problems.

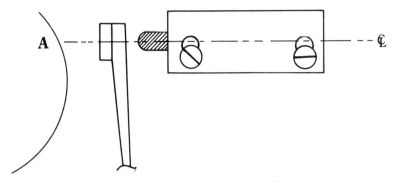

4-3 Hammer alignment—proper alignment.

Symptom   Printed characters appear faded at the top or bottom.

When a die strikes the platen, it should apply force evenly to produce a character of uniform contrast (Fig. 4-3). Over time, a hammer might fall slightly out of alignment and deliver excess force to the upper or lower portion of the die as shown in Figs. 4-4 and 4-5. This causes all characters to appear dull or faded where force drops off. Follow Procedure 4-2 to check and realign the hammer.

Symptom   The print head assembly moves back and forth across the page, but it does not print. The hammer does not fire, but a die rotates normally.

There are several possible causes for such symptoms, most of which relate to the hammer mechanism itself. If the hammer does not fire, it can be jammed, defective, or not receiving trigger signals from driver components within the printer's electronics. Procedure 4-3 walks you through a check of the hammer mechanism.

If your test readings from Procedure 4-3 indicate no problem with the hammer, it might not be receiving pulses (or pulses of sufficient amplitude) from its printer circuits. This might be because of defective wiring leading to the hammer, or a defective driver circuit in the electronics. Refer to chapter 6 for an explanation of printer electronics and troubleshooting.

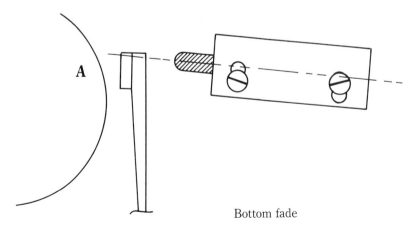

Bottom fade

4-4 Hammer alignment—bottom fade.

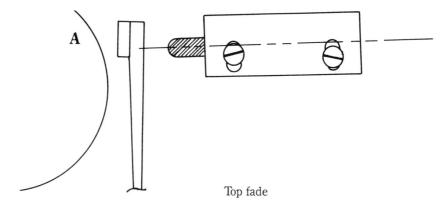

Top fade

4-5 Hammer alignment—top fade.

Symptom The print head assembly moves back and forth across the page, but print is light or nonexistent. The hammer does appear to fire.

Whenever you find light print, begin your investigation by checking the ribbon and ribbon advance, as well as the printwheel itself. If your ribbon is old or worn out, printing will be light regardless of how well the print head works. The same is true if it is not advancing with each character. If you find a problem with the ribbon advance, flip to chapter 7 for mechanical repairs. Also check for proper print wheel placement and orientation. Make sure the wheel is secure in its mounting bracket.

After you are satisfied that the ribbon and print wheel are intact, inspect the hammer using Procedure 4-3. If the hammer checks out, test the driver circuitry as outlined in chapter 6. Printer circuitry might not be providing pulses (or pulses with enough energy) to drive the hammer with normal force.

Symptom The print head assembly moves back and forth across the page, but print is intermittent. Characters might be jumbled.

Intermittent problems can sometimes be deceptive. Use procedure 4-4 to inspect the print head wiring for possible intermittent connections. One faulty wire can throw the entire assembly out of control.

It is also possible that a failure is occurring in the power supply. Marginal voltage levels can let the printer appear to operate, yet allow circuitry to act erratically. Check chapter 5 for a complete explanation of power supplies and troubleshooting.

Even if the power supply is functional, you still could have an intermittent condition in the electronic control package. Chapter 6 provides details and troubleshooting procedures for electronics circuits.

Dot-matrix printers

Impact dot-matrix print heads use a series of hardened metal wires (called *print wires*) to deliver a series of dots to the page surface. Figure 4-6 shows a 9-pin print head with wires 3 and 6 firing. The face on a dot-matrix print head might be flat, or it could be curved slightly to accommodate the curvature of the platen (Fig. 4-7). To ensure the very best dot quality, pins are ground flat and polished once they are

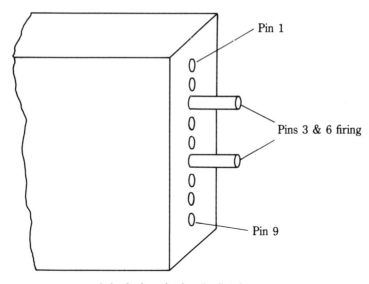

4-6 9-pin print head—flat face.

mounted in the head housing. As a result, print wires are not generally inter-
changeable without a loss of print quality. High-resolution print heads with 24 pins
are also commonly available and are assembled in essentially the same way.

Each pin is driven independently with a miniature solenoid as shown in Fig.
4-8. A print wire is fitted in the middle of each solenoid, or is driven through a
series of linkages by a remote solenoid. A brief electronic pulse from driver cir-

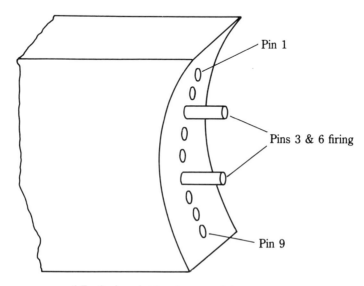

4-7 9-pin print head—curved face.

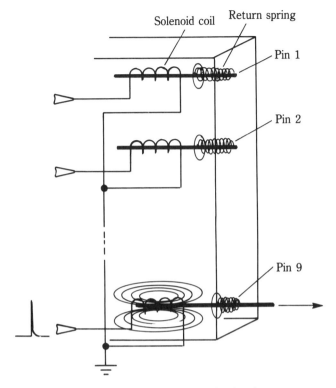

4-8 Impact dot-matrix print head.

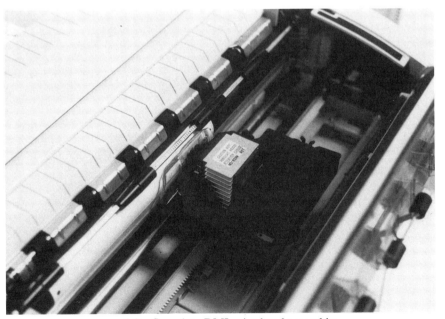

4-9 Complete DMI print head assembly.

cuits in the electronic control package creates an intense magnetic field through a coil. This, in turn, thrusts the print wire forward onto the ribbon and paper. When the pulse has passed, a spring return draws the pin back to its rest position within its solenoid. All of this can happen in excess of 300 times per second—faster than your eye can perceive. Figure 4-9 shows a complete dot-matrix impact print head assembly.

A great concern with impact dot-matrix printing is an eventual buildup of heat in the head housing. Each time a solenoid fires, energy contained in its driver pulse is given up as heat. With continuous use, heat builds up faster than it can be dissipated by a simple metal housing. This is especially true when printing bit-image graphics, when print wires fire continuously for prolonged periods of time. A *heat sink* composed of metal fins is often added to a print head housing, as in Fig. 4-9. This heat sink helps excess heat to be carried away by ambient (surrounding) air. If heat were left unchecked, the resulting expansion of metal parts would cause excessive friction and wear in the head assembly. In some cases, uneven expansion of pins within the housing may cause them to jam in either the extended or the retracted position. As a general rule, *never* touch a print head just after it finishes printing. Allow time for it to cool down.

Troubleshooting impact dot-matrix print heads

Symptom   The print head assembly moves back and forth across the page, but it does not print. None of the print wires appear to fire.

The most common source of trouble in moving-head printers is the wiring harness between the print head and driver circuits. Constant flexing in the wiring harness can eventually lead to wiring fatigue and breakage. This interrupts the signal and return (ground) paths that driver signals require. Procedure 4-5 gives you a general guide for wiring continuity tests. Each solenoid in a dot-matrix print head is driven independently through the wiring harness. If only one (or a few) print wires are failing, it is possible that only a portion of the cables is broken.

Heat buildup can be a problem with impact dot-matrix print heads. Extreme heating can cause metal parts to expand and jam print wires within their metal housing. Stop the printer and turn off all power. You can feel for overheating by holding your hand *over* the print head and letting heat convect upward through the air. *Never* touch a print head after it finishes printing (especially after a long printing run) or you might receive a nasty burn on your hand or fingers. Your particular print head might not get *that* hot—but you never know.

If you sense overheating, allow the print head to cool completely. Remove the print head from its carriage mount and examine each print wire. Make sure each wire still moves freely in and out. Cool print wires should move freely. If they do, test the printer again—it might be a wiring or driver problem. If they do not, your wires might be bent, worn, or clogged with dust and oils accumulated from long periods of use. You can attempt to clean and lubricate the print wires using preventive maintenance procedures in chapter 8. If this does not improve the print wires' freedom, replace the print head entirely.

Finally, driver circuits might be failing in the printer's electronic control package. They might not be producing trigger pulses (or pulses of sufficient energy) to fire each print wire. Refer to chapter 6 for explanations of electronic circuits and troubleshooting.

Symptom The print head moves back and forth across the page, but printing is intermittent. Wires appear to fire erratically.

Intermittent printing is common among all types of moving-head printers. The wiring harness that carries driver signals to a print head can fatigue over time, resulting in one or more intermittent connections. Follow Procedure 4-4 to check for intermittent wiring. Remember that the harness assembly might involve discrete wires, flexible ribbon wire, and a variety of connectors. Just be sure to check continuity from the driver circuits to the print head.

Symptom The print head fires, but there are one or more white (missing) or black lines through the print.

This type of problem is almost always located inside the print head mechanism itself. One or more missing lines (which gives the illusion of a white line) in the print suggests that a print wire is not firing. It might be bent or stuck inside its housing. Turn off all printer power, remove the head from its carriage mount, and check each wire to be sure it moves freely. If there is any resistance, you may attempt to clean the face and wire as described in chapter 8.

On the other hand, a black line suggests that a print wire is physically stuck in the extended position—either jammed or frozen by foreign matter. See if the wire moves at all. Some resistance from dust and oil buildup often can be cleared with careful cleaning and light lubrication. Otherwise, the head might have to be replaced.

If the print wires appear to be intact, their driving solenoids might be defective. Use Procedure 4-6 to check the solenoids in an impact dot-matrix printer. The procedure will help you to determine if a solenoid is open or short-circuited.

Another source of problems can occur in the wiring harness. An open signal line will prevent a solenoid from firing. Use Procedure 4-5 to check for broken wiring in the harness. A short circuit in the harness can cause a solenoid to fire when another solenoid fires, or stay on all the time. Procedure 4-7 guides you through a test for wiring shorts.

Symptom Printing is correct, but it appears faint.

Your first suspicion when faced with faint print should be the ribbon. Check the ribbon to be sure it is fresh and advancing properly as the carriage moves back and forth. Replace any ribbon that is exhausted or drying out. If the ribbon does not advance correctly, refer to chapter 7 for an explanation of mechanical systems and troubleshooting.

The print head might be too far away from the platen. Many printers offer an adjustment lever that allows you to alter the print head's distance from the platen. It allows the printer to accommodate various paper thicknesses. This lever might or might not be visible from the top cover. Even though this adjustment moves the head only a few thousandths of an inch, it can have a significant impact on print contrast. If an adjustment lever is not available, see chapter 7 for adjustment procedures.

Thermal

As you saw in chapter 1, thermal print heads are available in two forms: moving head and line-print head. The moving-head thermal dot-matrix print head is shown in Fig. 4-10. Although this type of thermal print head finds wide use in small, portable equipment applications, it is rarely (if ever) used for full-page commercial printers. Figure 4-11 illustrates a basic thermal line-print head. A thermal dot heater is available for every possible dot in a horizontal line. Line-print devices offer reliability and mechanical simplicity because a carriage mechanism is not needed to move the print head. Facsimile machines use line-print heads almost exclusively for full-page printing.

Although these two types of print heads might appear to be vastly different, they both use exactly the same principles (see Figs. 4-12 and 4-13). A driver circuit sends short, high-energy electrical pulses to each desired heater element. The heater element itself is little more than a resistor or semiconductor device formed onto the face of the print head. These small, low-mass elements can heat and cool again very quickly (on the order of several milliseconds). Energy contained in a driver pulse heats the desired element. This heat causes a corresponding dot to form on the thermal paper. After the driver pulse passes, the heater cools almost instantly.

Keep in mind that heating and cooling is *critical* to the proper operation of a thermal print head. If dot heaters do not cool quickly enough, printed dots might appear smeared in the direction of head movement. This limits the speed that a thermal printer can operate. In many cases, the heater is assembled onto a metal substrate (support) to aid in cooling.

Since a thermal print head is actually held in contact with the page surface, head tension is also very important. The head must exert enough pressure on the page to ensure a positive contact, yet not enough to restrict the paper's movement through the paper transport mechanism.

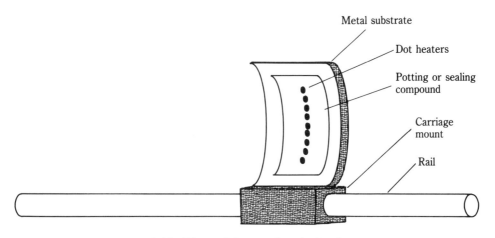

4-10 Thermal dot-matrix print head.

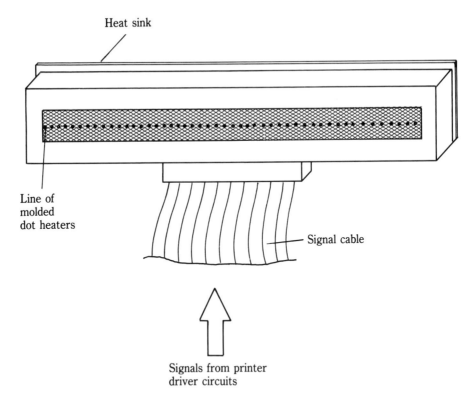

Heat sink

Line of
molded
dot heaters

Signal cable

Signals from printer
driver circuits

4-11   Thermal line-print head.

In actual operation, a moving-head thermal printer behaves almost exactly like an impact dot-matrix unit as shown in Fig. 4-14. Logic and driver circuits (although not *exactly* alike) are very similar in their structure and approach.

A thermal line-print head, however, is much more sophisticated in its operation. Logic must disassemble an entire row of print into rows of horizontal dots. The data representing that row is passed to driver circuitry, that *multiplexes* (or breaks up) the row into several sections (often one-fourth of the page), and sends each section in turn until the row is completed. Logic then computes the next horizontal row of dots, advances the paper by one dot width, and begins another printing cycle.

In practice, this is not quite as complicated as it might sound. Instead of printing a desired line of text characters as vertical columns of 9 or 24 dots (as a moving-head thermal printer does), the desired line of text is broken down into horizontal rows and printed one row at a time by the line-print head. Theoretically, you could print an entire row at a time, but this would require an incredibly large network of drivers and interconnecting wiring. Multiplexing the driver signals serves to reduce the size of the driver network, simplify interconnecting wiring, and reduce the surges of heat generated by the line head.

Dot heaters

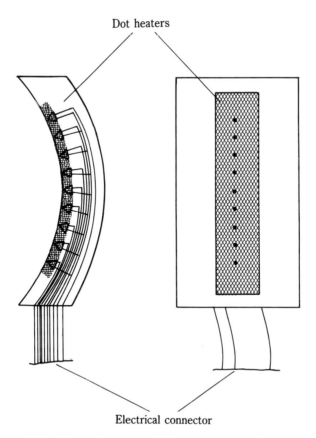

Electrical connector

4-12   Thermal print head diagram—moving head.

Dot heaters

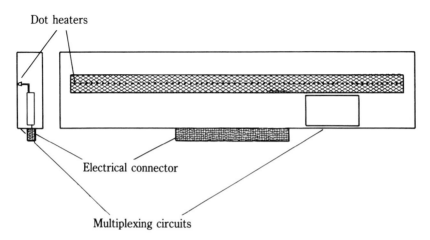

Electrical connector

Multiplexing circuits

4-13   Thermal print head diagram—line-print head.

4-14 Thermal print head in operation.

For the most part, thermal print heads of any type are *not* repairable. If a heater element should short or open, there is no way to remove the potting material to expose the failure. As a rule, thermal head problems fall into the same categories as impact dot-matrix devices; wiring to the head might be broken or intermittent, logic or driver circuitry might malfunction, or the head itself could be faulty. Replace any questionable print head.

Troubleshooting thermal print heads

Symptom   The paper and carriage (if used) advance normally, but the print is intermittent or nonexistent.

If there is no print at all, check the *paper!* Thermal paper is coated with heat-sensitive chemicals on one side ONLY. If paper is inserted so that the uncoated side contacts the print head, it simply will not work. Remember that thermal paper also has a limited life span (on the order of several years). Beyond that, heat-sensitive chemicals begin to degrade and discolor the paper. Always make sure that your paper supply is fresh and inserted correctly.

Begin your repair by investigating the wiring harness that connects driver circuitry to the print head assembly. Use Procedure 4-5 to check for broken wiring, and Procedure 4-4 to test for intermittent wiring. Pay special attention to any common or ground wires that you might find in the harness. If a common wire fails, it disables all of the heater elements.

If paper is fresh and wiring is satisfactory, inspect the driver circuitry as out-lined in chapter 6. Make sure the heater elements are receiving driver pulses. If all else fails, try replacing the print head.

Symptom   The paper and carriage (if used) advance normally, but there are white (missing) or black lines running through the print.

As with the impact dot-matrix print head, white or black lines suggest that a heater element is not firing, or is firing all the time. The cause can be rooted in a wiring harness problem, so try Procedure 4-7 to check for wiring shorts, or Proce-dure 4-5 to check for broken wiring. Remember that you will be measuring across resistive or semiconductor heater elements, so your readings might be different from those obtained from an impact dot-matrix head. If your readings appear inconclusive, disconnect the print head and repeat the test.

Examine your driver circuitry using procedures in chapter 6. One or more driver outputs might be open or shorted. Depending on whether your driver has failed in the on or off condition, it could be causing a black or white line (respec-tively) through the print. If all else fails, replace the print head itself. A heater ele-ment could be open or shorted.

Ink jet

Of all the various technologies used in printers, only ink jet printers do not place a print head in direct contact with the page in order to deliver images. This type of *noncontact* printing essentially sprays droplets of liquid ink onto the page to form the desired image.

As you learned in chapter 1, continuous flow ink jet printing is widely used in high-volume industrial marking systems. In this system, the print head remains stationary and surfaces to be printed are moved past it at a constant speed. Contin-uous flow systems are *not* well suited to home or office printers. They require a source of pressure and vacuum, as well as a large, bulky ink reservoir that must be filtered continuously. The maintenance and repair of continuous flow print heads is not covered in this book, but you should be aware that they exist.

The most widely used technique for ink jet printing is known as *drop-on-demand*, which means that ink droplets are generated only as they are needed. This is a very efficient method—since ink flows only as needed, only a small reser-voir of ink is required. In many cases, the reservoir is a disposable attachment that clips right onto the print head and can last for 500,000 characters or so.

Ejecting drops on demand, however, is not as obvious a process as impact printing. Consider that an ink jet print head must eject precisely measured drop-lets of indelible ink through nozzles thinner than a normal human hair at speeds that can exceed several hundred drops per second. Pumping action is handled by small piezoelectric crystals. Figure 4-15 shows a basic example of the piezoelectric effect. When a dc voltage is applied across a piezo crystal material, the crystal will oscillate (or vibrate) at one constant rate. Very small crystal "pumps" are mounted within each nozzle as illustrated in Fig. 4-16.

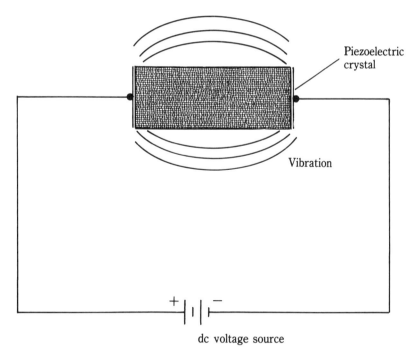

4-15 Piezoelectric effect.

Figure 4-16 shows the nozzle at rest and ready to fire. Notice that the piezo crystal is not oscillating. When a driver pulse is applied to the crystal, it begins to deflect. As the crystal deflects inward (as in Fig. 4-17) it squeezes the ink channel and applies a sudden pressure that launches a single droplet. The crystal then moves in the other direction. This creates a vacuum that draws additional ink into

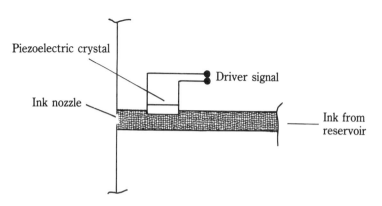

4-16 Ink jet operation—nozzle ready to fire.

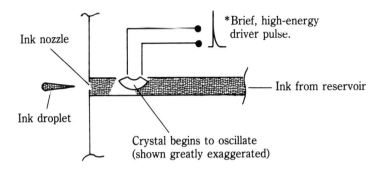

4-17   Ink jet operation—nozzle fires.

the channel as in Fig. 4-18. At this point, the driver pulse is over, so the crystal rests and awaits another pulse.

Ink droplets can also be developed using the *bubble-jet* method. In this method, piezoelectric crystals are replaced by small heating elements that heat ink in the channel as shown in Fig. 4-19. As with the piezo system, ink normally fills the channel, but is stopped by the restriction of the small nozzle. A driver pulse causes a ring heater to evenly heat ink within the channel. An air bubble forms, and expands (Fig. 4-20), and finally bursts. This pushes a droplet of ink out of the nozzle. The sudden ejection of ink causes a vacuum which draws more ink into the channel as shown in Fig. 4-21. Another droplet could then be fired.

As with thermal print heads, ink jet print heads are sealed units that cannot be opened for repair. If a crystal breaks or a heater fails, the entire head assembly must be replaced. Cleaning is virtually the only procedure that can be performed on ink jet heads. Printer ink is solvent-based, so it is not very sensitive to the open air. Ink jet print heads do not clog quickly, but eventually the solvent evaporates and leaves ink sediment to clog the nozzles. As long as ink flows during regular

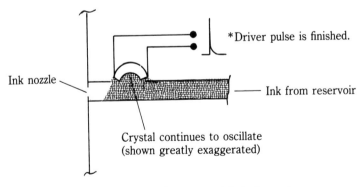

4-18   Ink jet operation—more ink is drawn in.

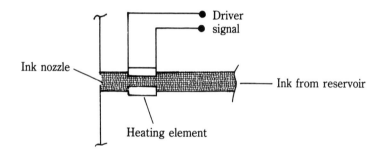

4-19 Bubble jet operation—nozzle ready to fire.

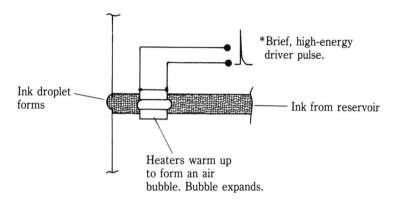

4-20 Bubble jet operation—bubble forms and expands.

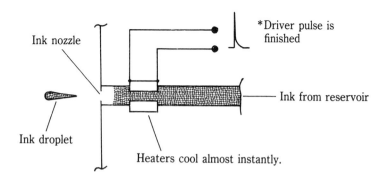

4-21 Bubble jet operation—nozzle fires; more ink is drawn in.

use, this should not become a problem, but after long periods of disuse (more than several weeks) a clog could occur.

In most cases, clogs can be cleared simply by wiping off the face of each nozzle, or by applying gentle force to the ink supply container. Avoid using water or harsh solvents of any type unless suggested specifically by your printer's manufacturer. More serious jams might require introducing a cleaning solvent solution to the ink channels. Refer to chapter 8 for general guidelines to ink jet care and cleaning.

Troubleshooting ink jet print heads

Symptom   The printer head assembly moves back and forth, but it does not print, or it only prints intermittently.

If there is no print at all, check your ink supply. Figure 4-22 shows a full ink bladder. Even though there may still appear to be ink remaining in the reservoir as shown in Fig. 4-23, there might not be enough to fill each of the ink channels. Replace the ink carriage to ensure a fresh ink supply.

Check for clogged ink nozzles. An ink jet printer that has not been used for long periods of time might be clogged from dried ink in its channels. A severe case of clogging can block all of the nozzles. Refer to cleaning instructions specified in your owner's manual, or refer to chapter 8 for general cleaning techniques.

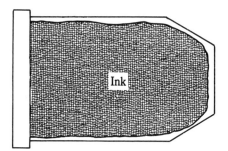

4-22   Ink cartridge—full ink bladder.

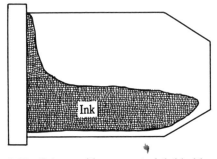

4-23   Ink cartridge—empty ink bladder.

If your ink supply is fresh and clear, use Procedure 4-5 to check for broken wires in the print head wiring harness. Use the procedure just as you would for any of the other print heads in this chapter. Remember to look for any common conductors in the harness. A break here could disable the entire print head. Intermittent printing might be the result of an intermittent connection in the wiring harness. Use Procedure 4-4 to check for intermittent connections.

Ink pumps (either piezoelectric or thermal) require substantial voltage pulses to operate. These pulses are generated through driver circuits in the printer's electronic control package. Refer to chapter 6 for troubleshooting electronic circuitry.

Finally, when all else fails, the problem might reside in the print head itself. Try replacing the print head.

Symptom   The print head assembly moves back and forth, but there are one or more white (missing) or black lines running through the print.

A white line appearing consistently through print (or graphics) suggests that a nozzle is clogged. A jammed ink nozzle can often be cleared simply by wiping the front face of the print head, or applying gentle force to the ink supply. Review your manufacturer's procedures, or those outlined in chapter 8, for clearing jammed ink nozzles.

An open circuit in the print head's wiring harness might account for the missing line. Use Procedure 4-4 to inspect the wiring harness for open circuits. If there are black lines running through the print, there could an internal short circuit in the harness. See Procedure 4-7 to evaluate any possible shorts in the harness.

An electronic fault in your driver circuits can account for these symptoms as well. Refer to chapter 6 for an explanation of electronic operations and troubleshooting. Finally, try replacing the print head assembly.

Symptom   The print is faint or smudged.

Check your paper! In order for ink jet printing to work correctly, liquid ink must be absorbed into the paper fast enough to dry almost instantly. Not all papers absorb ink formulations readily, so ink might smudge as the head moves across the page, or when you handle the finished page with your hands. Some papers work just the opposite way and absorb ink so quickly and completely that images appear faint. Papers coated with clay or special chemicals intended to react with ink formulations are usually preferred for ink jet printing applications. Typical ink jet paper appears smooth and shiny on one side, while the other side appears dull and textured like normal page.

Not every clog is a complete one. A partially-clogged ink nozzle could interfere with the ink path, causing droplets to spatter and appear smudged on the printout. Try wiping the face of the print head to clear away any congealed ink.

Electrostatic

Electrostatic (ES) printers are fundamentally different from the other types of printing technologies that you have learned about. Dot formation is not a simple, one-step process as with impact, thermal, or ink-jet technologies. Instead, an image is formed by a complex interaction of light, static electricity, chemistry, and heat, all guided by an electronic control package that is much more powerful than those in previously described printers.

Because of this complexity, it is hard to define precisely what the ES print head *is*. A "print head" has been defined already as a device used to transfer a processed image to a page surface. No one device in the electrostatic printer is capable of performing this function alone. A number of independent devices acting together is needed to accomplish this feat. These devices are commonly known as the *image formation system* (IFS), and will be considered the print head of an ES printer. Figure 4-24 is a simplified diagram of a typical IFS that illustrates its eight general parts: photosensitive drum, cleaning blade, erase lamp assembly, primary corona, writing mechanism, toner, transfer corona, and fusing rollers.

The heart of the IFS is a continuously rotating metal drum coated with a delicate photosensitive material. The drum receives an image from a "writing mechanism," picks up opaque toner to develop the image, then transfers the developed image to paper. Although you might think that this constitutes a print head (since

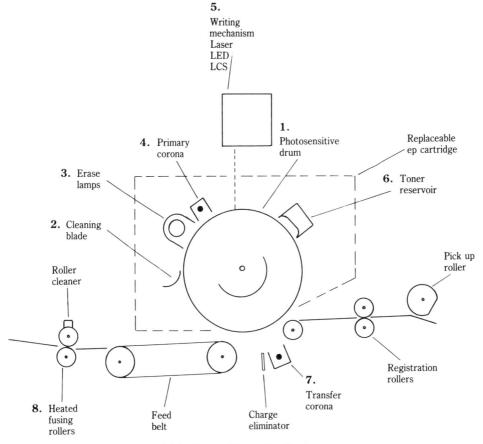

4-24 Image Formation System.

it delivers a processed image to a page surface), none of that would be possible without help from the corona wires, writing mechanism, or fusing rollers.

A printing cycle actually begins with both physical and electrical *cleaning*. It might seem like a rather unimportant step, but a drum does not transfer every granule of toner perfectly every time. Remaining granules must be scraped away by physical cleaning, or they could be transferred onto subsequent pages, resulting in some of the random black "speckles" that you might see on the page from time to time. A scraper, which is little more than a glorified squeegee, must remove as much toner as possible without scratching or nicking the photosensitive drum surface. Any imperfections on the drum are *permanent*, and show up on every subsequent page until the drum is replaced by changing the EP cartridge.

Electrical cleaning is performed by a series of intense erase lamps placed in close proximity to the drum. Recall from chapter 1 that a drum surface contains electrical charges corresponding to dots that compose the image to be printed. These changes remain after toner has been transferred, and must be erased completely before a new image can be written onto the drum. An intense light source of the proper wavelength dissipates any charges on the drum and "clears the slate" for a new image.

On the erased parts of the drum, the surface is electrically neutral (erasure is a continuous process, so only areas of the drum immediately exposed to the erasure

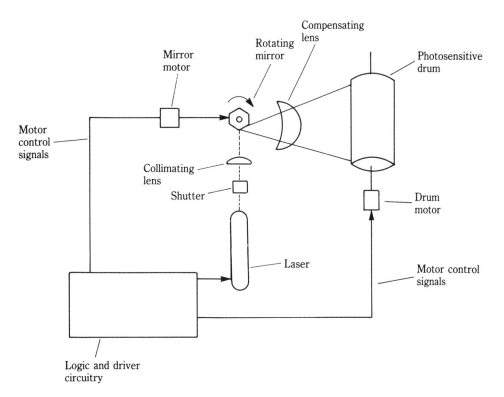

4-25 Laser image system.

lamps become neutral). However, a neutral drum does not react to light signals from the writing mechanism. An initial (or primary) charge must be applied to the drum surface. This is the task of the *primary corona*. The primary corona is little more than a wire carrying a very high voltage. An electrical field produced by this high voltage places a uniform charge across the drum. At this point, the drum is still empty, but it is now ready to accept dot patterns from a writing mechanism.

A *writing mechanism* projects horizontal rows of dots precisely as required over the moving drum to form the characters and graphics that utltimately appear on the page. Laser beams have been the primary writing mechanism since electrostatic printers were first introduced. Figure 4-25 shows a basic laser writing mechanism. As the printer's main logic calculates each dot in a horizontal scan, it fires the laser into a rotating hexagonal mirror. If you are familiar with geometry, you might see that a laser beam is reflected from mirror to drum at an angle that increases as the mirror rotates. Logic signals shutter the laser beam on and off to coincide with the presence or absence of dots. Mirror rotation is timed so that one sweep across the drum places an entire row of dots as needed. This is called a *sweep* or *scan line*. When a photon of laser light strikes the surface of a charged drum, that point on the surface becomes properly charged to attract toner. Points not exposed to laser light do not attract toner. When a sweep is complete, driver circuits advance the drum for another sweep.

This type of system can place up to 300 dots per inch (dpi) with reasonable accuracy. With such a complex and delicate system of optics, however, any shift in

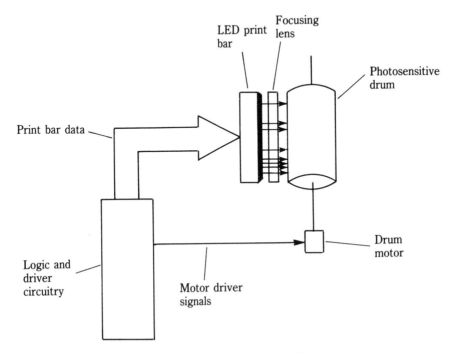

4-26   Typical print bar assembly.

alignment over time introduces severe distortion into the image. These difficulties have kept laser-writing mechanisms expensive and out of reach of many consumers. Line-printing heads consisting of light-emitting diodes (LEDs) or liquid crystal shutters (LCSs) lend simplicity and reliability to the system as shown in Fig. 4-26. They can also deliver light-dots to a charged drum, but they last longer, are almost totally immune to shock and vibration, and can be realigned far more easily.

After exposure by a writing mechanism, the image (now placed on the drum as dots of static electricity) must be developed with *toner*. Toner is basically an extremely fine powder of iron, plastic, and organic compounds that is easily attracted by static electricity. When the exposed drum passes a trough of toner, charged areas attract toner. Other areas remain clean. As the drum picks up toner, a fresh page of paper is picked up and positioned between two registration rollers.

Paper does not actually contact the drum. Toner is literally pulled by a static charge on the paper that is stronger than the charge holding toner on the drum. Paper is charged with a second corona wire known as *transfer corona*. Paper is transported along with the rotating drum and toner is attracted to the paper. This places the drum's image on the paper. Ideally, all toner particles are attracted, but in reality, some granules remain. Leftover drum toner is removed by the cleaning blade in preparation for another page.

Although the image is on paper now, it is not yet permanent—toner is still in its powder form. A feeding belt carries the page to a set of heated *fusing rollers*. Heat and pressure melt toner and bind it permanently into the fiber of the page. Finally, a finished page arrives at the output tray.

In spite of the added complexity that an Image Formation System offers, many common problems can be traced quickly and easily. Before you review the following troubleshooting procedures, however, take a minute to memorize two very important safety considerations for electrostatic printers.

- *Beware of high voltage*! Remember from chapter 3 that high voltages can be potentially lethal under the right conditions. Your multimeter leads might not offer enough insulation to protect you from these voltages.

- *Use extreme caution with laser light*! Although most lasers are low-power devices, a direct beam at the proper wavelength can inflict serious and permanent damage to your eyes. *Never* look directly into a laser tube or diode while printer power is on! Even invisible beams working above the range of human vision can seriously impair your vision. No repair is worth your eyesight!

Troubleshooting electrostatic image formation systems

Symptom Printed images are faint, light, or appear washed out.

In many instances, toner powder might no longer be distributed evenly within its disposable EP cartridge. As toner is drawn away during printing, remaining toner might be too far away to be sufficiently attracted. If insufficient toner is attracted, images can appear light or washed out. This can also happen to sections of the toner cartridge (e.g., left half, right half, middle, etc.), and is a typical prelude to toner exhaustion. Follow Procedure 4-8 to check the EP cartridge.

Check both of your corona wires using Procedure 4-9. Remember that electrostatic printers need substantial levels of static electricity to function. Corona wires are high-voltage leads that provide electric charge fields to the drum and paper. The primary corona charges the drum, while the transfer corona places a charge on paper. If these wires should become corroded or dirty, they might not be able to support an even charge across their full length. A partially or fully washed out image may result.

Finally, it is possible that the high-voltage portion of your power supply might be defective. If there is insufficient voltage potential, both coronas will be unable to generate appropriate electric fields. You could follow the explanations and troubleshooting procedures for power supplies contained in chapter 5, but due to the inherent dangers of high-voltage testing, you might wish simply to replace the high-voltage supply outright.

Symptom   Printed images are excessively dark or all black.

The contrast of an image is largely a function of toner transfer. Where an image is very light, too little toner is reaching the paper. A very dark image often results from too much toner. There may be several reasons why an image is too dark. Start by checking the printer's contrast (or intensity) control. It may be set too dark, especially after you install a fresh EP cartridge. Check the distribution of toner as outlined in Procedure 4-8. Once in a great while, you may encounter a defective EP cartridge. If you cannot correct excessive darkness by redistributing toner or adjusting print intensity, try replacing the EP cartridge.

A problem may exist in your primary corona wire. If the electric charging field is too high, the drum may be oversensitized and attract too much toner. Examine and clean your corona wires as outlined in Procedure 4-9. If you are unable to clean the primary corona for any reason, replace the EP cartridge.

Overcharging can also be caused by an excessive power supply voltage. If you wish to follow the guidelines in chapter 5, you may check the voltage levels leaving the high voltage supply, but due to the inherent dangers of high-voltage supplies, you may wish simply to replace the suspect power supply.

Symptom   Printing intensity is correct, but random smudges are occurring.

In almost all cases, you can attribute smudges to one or more dirty areas within the IFS. Excess toner can accumulate after long periods of use, or as the cartridge becomes worn out. Suspect the drum first if you see an accumulation of toner at the page sides. Since the drum is part of the EP cartridge, the entire cartridge must be replaced to exchange a drum.

One or more rollers might be dirty. Turn off printer power and allow fusing rollers to cool. Examine all rollers and belts in the paper path thoroughly. Clean any dirty rollers with a soft cloth dampened (if necessary) with water *only*. Never use chemical detergents or solvents on rubber rollers. Dry each roller *thoroughly* before retesting the printer. If you notice repeated buildup on the fusing rollers, check their heater wiring to ensure that each roller is grounded properly.

Symptom   Print appears to be correct, but there are white (light) or black strips along the length of the page, or "speckles" that appear consistently on every page.

This almost always points to a defect in the photosensitive drum. Remember that the drum's surface coating is extremely sensitive and delicate. Any foreign matter on the paper or paper path can scratch or pit the drum. Once this coating is comprised, it cannot be repaired, so replace the EP cartridge.

Speckles can also be caused by a defective fusing assembly. If fusing rollers do not get hot enough, toner will not melt fully into the paper. Unmelted toner can be picked up by the fusing roller only to rub off later on subsequent pages. A clear sign of poor fusing is an image that you can smudge with your fingers—toner is still in the powder form. Check the wiring to the fusing rollers after your printer is off and fusing rollers have cooled completely. It might be necessary for you to replace the fusing roller.

If your printer uses an LED or LCS print bar instead of a laser, one or more of the LED or LCS light points may be defective, resulting in an unwanted absence or presence of dots. Driver circuitry that operates the print bars may also be defective, but driver circuitry is covered in chapter 6.

Symptom Images appear to be distorted. They might appear too short, too tall, wavy, or light and out of focus.

Images are scanned onto a continuously moving drum using an optical writing mechanism such as a laser. If a drum motor problem occurs, it can interfere with the drum rotation rate. Images might appear stretched or compressed vertically as the motor jumps around, while their horizontal spacing remains unaffected. Observe your drum's rotation and check for any obstructions. If you see rotation problems but cannot find an obstruction, try replacing the drive motor.

Scanning problems can result in waves, loss of focus, left or right image shifting, or other types of anomaly. In this case, the rotating mirror might be out of alignment (rotating improperly) or obstructed. Optical components might be defective, dirty, or out of alignment. The laser itself might also be failing. If you suspect an alignment or laser problem, return the printer to the manufacturer for service. It is almost impossible to access and align laser printer optics "by eye." Luckily, electrostatic printers using LED or LCS print bars are much more resistant to alignment and dust problems than their laser predecessors.

Troubleshooting procedures

○ **Procedure 4-1** Check and clean the print wheel.

Begin by removing the print wheel from its mounting clip. It could simply be pushed into place, or locked down by a screw or secondary clip. Examine each petal arm carefully for cracks in the plastic or other signs of fatigue. Replace any print wheel that shows signs of impending breakage.

Clean each die carefully by using a stiff toothbrush soaked with water and mild household detergent. This cleaning action tends to spatter water and debris everywhere, so keep your work well away from the printer. Check the dies often to see that they are cleaning up well. When all dies are cleaned, dry every petal and die very carefully (especially any metal clips that hold the die in place) and replace the wheel in the printer. It might also be a good idea to install a fresh ribbon to give your print a clean, crisp appearance.

○ **Procedure 4-2**   Align the hammer.

The hammer mechanism is generally visible on top of the print wheel motor. Its striking surface must be parallel to the print wheel. If it is not, striking force will not be even across the die, and characters might appear faded. While its horizontal alignment (left or right) is often fixed, its vertical alignment (up or down) can shift with time or physical abuse.

Align the hammer by loosening its adjustment screws (just enough to move the hammer—nothing more), then shifting its orientation as shown in Fig. 4-3. You can align a hammer by eye—its setting is not too critical. Retest the printer and tweak your adjustment if necessary.

◐ **Procedure 4-3**   Check the hammer resistance.

A hammer is subjected to sudden, sharp impacts on a continuous basis. Eventually, its plunger can jam or its solenoid can fail. Start your test by turning off printer power. Inspect the plunger and see that it moves freely within its housing (though you might feel tension from its spring-return). If it does not move freely, you should replace the hammer mechanism.

If the plunger moves freely, examine solenoid resistance with your ohmmeter as shown in Fig. 4-27. Check along the hammer's outer housing to find any optimum resistance ratings. For an ordinary solenoid, you will measure between 10 and 100 ohms (some solenoids might measure more). A reading of infinity suggests that the solenoid is open. A very low reading suggests that the solenoid is internally shorted. In either case, replace the hammer assembly immediately. If the solenoid is all right, it might not be receiving pulses correctly from driver circuitry.

◐ **Procedure 4-4**   Check for intermittent wiring.

Test the continuity of each wire connecting your print head to the electronics control package. Essentially, this means measuring the resistance of each wire and looking for a very low resistance (ideally a short circuit). This indicates that the wire is connected. In order to ensure a comprehensive reading, measure from the print head right to the drivers—get as close as you can. Wiggle the wiring all the way along the harness to stimulate any intermittent connection. An intermittent connec-

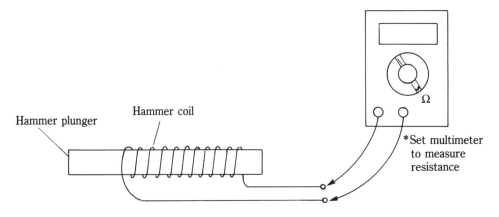

4-27   Check the hammer.

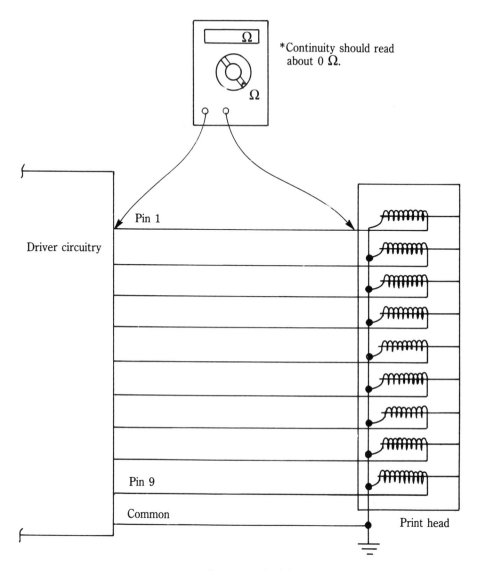

4-28 Check head wiring.

tion causes your resistance reading to bounce around erratically between zero and infinity. Replace or repair any questionable wiring.

Be careful not to confuse intermittent wiring with intermittent measurement. Test leads that are not connected properly can also exhibit symptoms or an intermittent connection.

Procedure 4-5 Check for broken wiring.

This is a continuity check of all harness wiring between your print head and driver circuitry as shown in Fig. 4-28. Turn off all printer power and measure the resistance of each conductor in the harness. Remember your harness might be

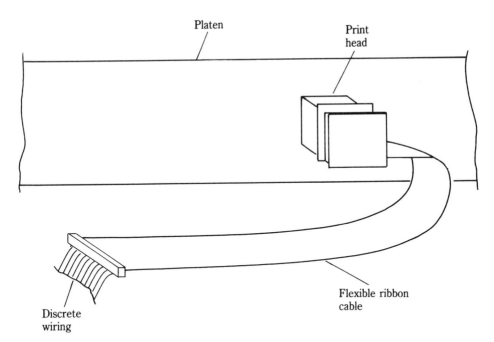

Platen

Print head

Flexible ribbon cable

Discrete wiring

4-29 Typical print head wiring.

built from several different types of conductors. For example, most print heads use a flexible ribbon cable from the head to the printer's base, then complete the driver connections with discrete wiring. This is illustrated in Fig. 4-29.

A properly connected conductor measures about zero ohms, while a broken conductor reads infinity. Wiggle each conductor to check for intermittent connections. One or more wires are often ground or common leads. If any of these are defective, they can easily interrupt the entire print head's operation. As with any other measurements, be sure your test probes are connected properly. Faulty test leads can fool you into seeing a problem that is not there.

◉ **Procedure 4-6** Check the print solenoids.

Measure resistance across each solenoid in the print head as shown in Fig. 4-30. You might have to remove the print head and disconnect it from its wiring harness. A working solenoid typically exhibits a resistance from 5 to 50 ohms. An infinite resistance measurement suggests an open solenoid, while a very low reading can indicate a shorted solenoid. In either case, the print head is defective and should be replaced.

◉ **Procedure 4-7** Check the print head and harness for short circuits.

Use your multimeter to test for short circuits in your print head and harness wiring. Measure across each pair of wire combinations as shown in Fig. 4-31. This can be a time-consuming process if there are a large number of harness wires. Although the resistance between wires might appear low due to the characteristic resistance of the print element (solenoid, heater, crystal, etc.), a dead short at

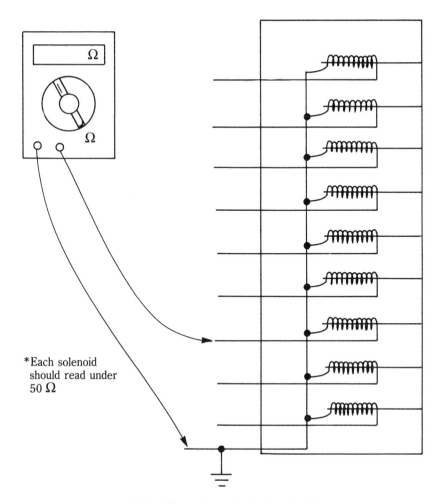

4-30 Measuring print head solenoids.

about 0 ohms indicates a serious problem. You might have to separate individual wires and try to find the source of your short circuit.

Remove and disconnect the print head and repeat your measurement. If you still read a short, your trouble probably rests somewhere in the wiring or driver circuits. If the short circuit reading disappears, however, one or more elements in the print head could be faulty, so it might have to be replaced.

○ **Procedure 4-8** Check the toner cartridge.

Remove the EP cartridge from your printer. You can refer to the printer manual for cartridge removal and replacement instructions. Typically, the cartridge contains a toner supply, a main corona, and a photosensitive drum, so be very careful when handling it. Do *not* touch the drum or corona wire. Gently rock the cartridge back and forth to redistribute the remaining toner. Reinsert the EP cartridge

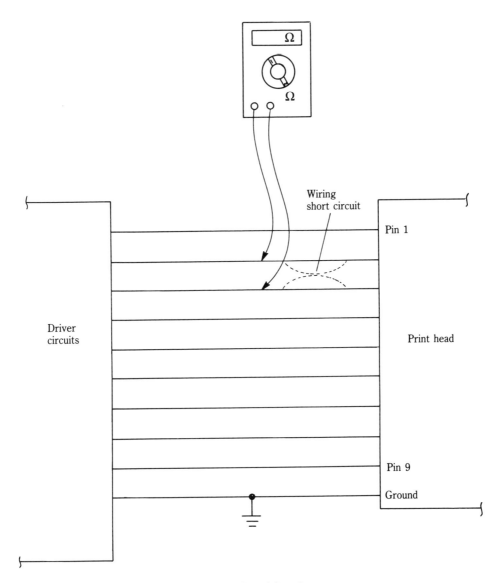

4-31 Check for wiring shorts.

and test your printer again. You might have to adjust the printing intensity control to optimize image contrast. If the image remains light or washed out, your toner supply could be exhausted or defective, so replace the EP cartridge.

⬤ **Procedure 4-9** Clean the corona wires.

Corona wires must be cleaned periodically to maintain an even electrical field between the wires and the drum (or paper). The primary corona is located in the EP cartridge, and the transfer corona is just below the drum's position at the printer's base.

Cleaning is a straightforward procedure. If your printer already comes with a specialized corona cleaning tool, follow the instructions outlined in your owner's manual. If you do not have such a tool available, use a dry cotton swab gently to brush away any corrosion or residue that has built up on the coronas. Brush gently but firmly. Be careful not to break the wire, or any fabric wrapping that might surround it.

Chapter 5

Power supplies

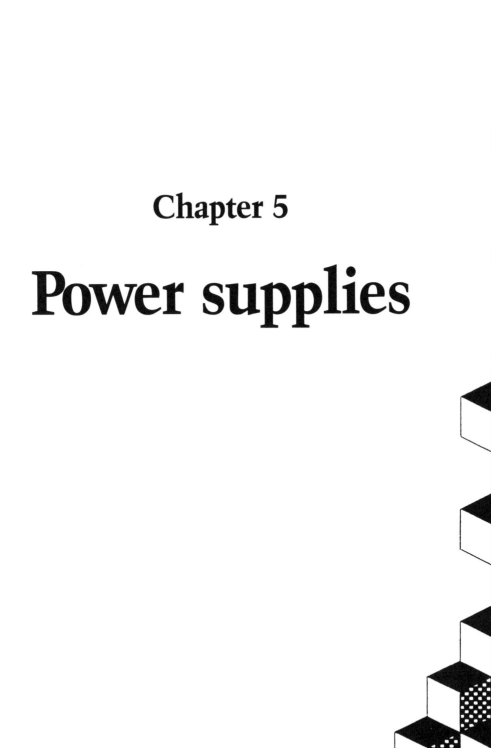

All electrical and electronic components inside your printer require a precise, stable source of voltage and current in order to operate correctly. This is not only true for printers, but for any piece of electronic equipment. In this chapter, you will learn the major components and operations of basic power supplies.

What a power supply is

In spite of its name, a power supply does not actually create a source of power all by itself. More accurately, it is a power *converter* which accepts commercial ac power available from any wall outlet, and converts it into a variety of low dc voltages that are used to power other circuits. Many electronic circuits require 5-, 12-, and 24-volt sources, but some supplies may provide secondary ac voltages to operate electromechanical equipment such as heavy-duty motors or solenoids.

Supply failures can manifest themselves in several (sometimes bizarre) ways. Complete failures where your supply is not producing any output at all are usually fast and straightforward repairs (e.g., a blown fuse or other obvious defect). Partial or intermittent failures, however, can be more obscure since power indicators are often lit and portions of the printer appear operational—at least intermittently. Some supply problems can even damage delicate electronics. Review the hazards of high-voltage that are outlined in chapter 3.

A power supply is generally a rugged and reliable device—so much so that they are often overlooked as possible problem sources. Remember that electronic circuits can not work properly (if at all) unless there is adequate voltage and current. Luckily, you can troubleshoot most general-purpose power supplies quickly and easily. Before you learn to troubleshoot a power supply, you should review their components and operations.

Supply components and operation

The four major segments of every power supply are shown in Fig. 5-1: *transformer, rectifier, filter,* and *regulator*. Each of these segments can utilize different components that vary in size and performance from supply to supply, but the concepts and operating principles of each segment are the same.

Transformers

Transformers are basically ac voltage converters. Their purpose is to convert ac line voltage entering the printer into another level of ac that the power supply can use. Most power supplies use a lower ac voltage than is available from an ordinary outlet, so a *step-down* transformer is used to reduce the line voltage (typically 115 volts ac) to a lower level such as 8-, 12-, or 18-volts ac.

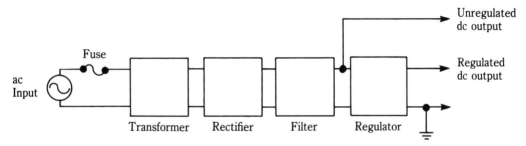

5-1 Power supply block diagram.

All transformers work on the premise of magnetic coupling as shown in the schematic diagram of Fig. 5-2. Input ac voltage (called *primary voltage*) is applied to the primary winding of the transformer. Current in the primary winding will produce a varying magnetic force field through the winding. Magnetic force is concentrated by a core material and carried to the secondary winding. A core is not mandatory—magnetic force can couple two coils through an air gap, but a *permeable core* (metal that can be magnetized) ensures the maximum concentration of force between primary and secondary coils.

The fluctuating magnetic field induces a secondary voltage across the secondary winding that is directly proportional to the ratio of primary-to-secondary windings. For example, if there are 1000 turns of wire in the primary winding and 100 turns of wire in the secondary winding, the ratio (or *turns ratio*) is 10:1. Since there are fewer turns in the secondary, the transformer of Fig. 5-2 is a *step-down* transformer. If 120 volts ac were applied to the primary of Fig. 5-2, a 10:1 step down would yield 12 volts ac output across the secondary. If the situation were reversed, the transformer would be a 1:10 *step-up* device. A transformer with an equal turns ratio would be considered an *isolation* device.

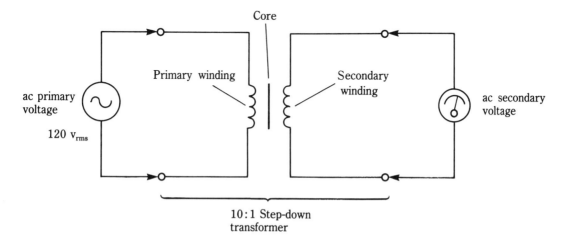

5-2 Basic transformer diagram.

Current is also stepped in a transformer, but it is stepped in reverse to the voltage ratio. If voltage is stepped down, current is stepped up by the same ratio, and vice versa. In this way, power taken from the transformer's secondary will roughly equal the power provided to the primary.

Due to magnetic core losses and resistance in the secondary winding, power developed in the secondary is actually somewhat less than power to the primary. In the example of Fig. 5-2, if a voltage source of 120 volts ac provided 0.1 amperes of current to the primary, primary power would be [P = I*V] 120 volts × 0.1 amps = 12 watts. With a step-down turns ratio of 10:1, the secondary voltage is 12 volts and the current is stepped up to 1 amp. Ideally, output power would be 12 volts × 1 amp = 12 watts, so output power would equal input power. In reality, there is slightly less than 12 watts out. You never get more power out than you put in.

You might wonder why transformers will not step dc voltage. After all, dc does produce strong magnetic fields in solenoids (such as those used for impact print wires). While this is true, a magnetic field must *fluctuate* over time in order to induce a potential (voltage) on another coil. DC magnetizes the primary winding, but without fluctuation, no voltage is induced across the secondary winding.

Some types of motors are built for ac, so they may be driven from the secondary output without further conversion to dc. These types of motors are very rare in commercial printers, so this chapter assumes there is only dc output from the supply.

Rectifiers

Secondary voltage from a transformer is always in an ac form. Although its output voltage may be stepped down significantly from the primary input, ac is totally unusable as a power source by electronic components such as integrated circuits. The process of *rectification* converts an ac signal into a pulsating dc signal. Even though the rectifier's output may vary greatly, its output signal remains in one

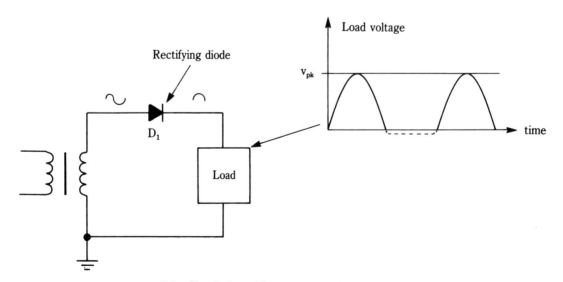

5-3 Classical rectifier stages—half-wave rectifier.

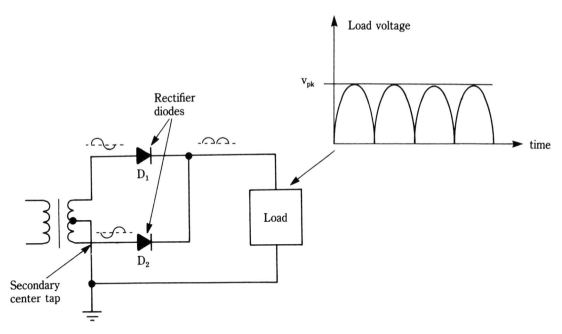

5-4 Classical rectifier stages—full-wave rectifier.

polarity—thus the term *pulsating dc*. You will encounter three classical types of rectifier circuits: half-wave, full-wave, and diode bridge. Each type is shown in Fig. 5-3 through 5-5.

A half-wave rectifier is shown in Fig. 5-3. It is the simplest and most straightforward type of rectifier, since it requires only one diode. The disadvantage to this

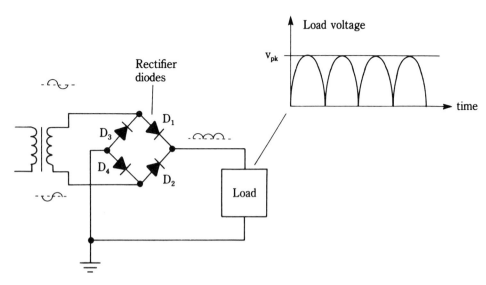

5-5 Classical rectifier stages—bridge rectifier.

circuit is that it is inefficient. It only rectifies one half of the ac signal—the other half is ignored and wasted. This leaves a gap between pulses which results in a lower average output voltage and a high amount of ac noise (or ripple) riding on that output. Half-wave rectifiers are not generally used in printer power supplies, but you should be aware of their existence.

Full-wave rectifiers such as the one in Fig. 5-4 offer significant advantages over the half-wave circuit. By using two diodes, both polarities of the secondary ac voltage may be rectified into pulsating dc. With little gap between pulses, the average output voltage is higher, while the ripple content of the dc signal is lower. As a result, power supplies that use full-wave rectifiers can generally support larger circuit loads. A disadvantage to the full-wave design is its transformer requirement. A center-tapped secondary winding is needed to supply a ground reference point. Such transformers are often larger and more expensive. This is unpopular with commercial printers striving to reduce size and weight.

Diode bridge rectifiers provide full-wave rectification without the trouble of a center-tapped transformer. Figure 5-5 shows a bridge rectifier. Notice how the bridge provides its own ground reference for the remainder of the power supply. This is by far the most popular type of rectifier. You can expect to see this approach taken in most printer power supplies.

Filters

By strict technical definition, pulsating dc *is* dc, but it is still unsuitable for even the most basic electronic power source. Pulses must be smoothed out over time to provide the steady dc that your printer electronics will need.

A *filter* acts to smooth out pulsating dc as illustrated in Fig. 5-6. One or more electrolytic power capacitors ranging in value from about 220 μF to 4700 μF are placed in a parallel across the rectifier's pulsating dc output. Since a capacitor is an energy storage device, it charges to the peak of the pulsating dc (Vpk), then tries to hold that charge to keep dc voltage steady.

As a pulse drops back down, the capacitor begins to discharge and supply current to keep a circuit functioning. As Fig. 5-6 shows, a light load (drawing little

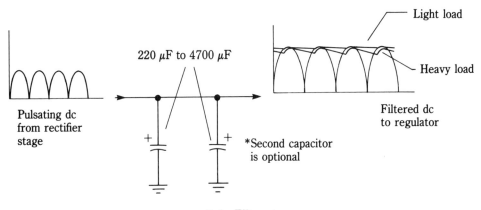

5-6 Filter stage.

current) discharges the filter only slightly, while a heavy load (requiring more current) discharges the filter more deeply between pulses.

When the next pulse of dc arrives from the rectifier, it charges the filter capacitor(s) once again to restore peak voltage. The amount that a filter's output varies between pulses becomes the value of *ripple*. Ideally, ripple should be zero—dc should be perfectly smooth like a battery's voltage. In reality, though, there is always some amount of ac ripple riding on the dc output.

Theoretically, as filter capacitance increases, ripple should decrease. This is true in practice, but there are some practical limits to how much capacitance can be used in a power filter. Size is always a big concern. Capacitors larger than 4700 μF tend to be very large and cumbersome. Large capacitors can also hold their charge for a long time, so there is often a shock hazard to consider. If you touch the leads of a charged capacitor, current flows through your body. Be very careful when working around charged capacitors.

Above 10,000 μF, a capacitor accepts so much current from the rectifier in its initial start-up (known as *inrush current*) that it may appear to be a short circuit to the power supply. This can trip the fuse or even damage the rectifier, so you rarely see more than 10,000 μF of filter capacitance in a power supply without some sort of current surge protection.

When you work on a power supply, it is a good idea to discharge any large capacitors before performing major work. Some supplies may already use *bleeder*

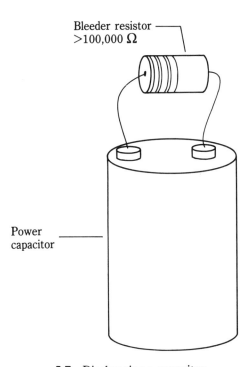

Bleeder resistor
>100,000 Ω

Power
capacitor

5-7 Discharging a capacitor.

resistors across each filter capacitor to automatically discharge the supply. Bleeder resistors are large values (often on the order of several mega-ohms). This ensures that there is always some small load on the filter. Use a 100 kilo-ohm resistor of your own to discharge any capacitor you are unsure about, as shown in Fig. 5-7. *Never* discharge a capacitor with a wire or screwdriver blade. The sudden release of energy can weld the screwdriver right to the capacitor's terminals, as well as damage its internal structure.

Regulators

A transformer, rectifier, and filter form the absolute essentials of every power supply. These parts combined successfully convert ac into dc. The trouble with this type of supply, however, is its ripple and lack of stable output voltage as ac input voltage or load demand changes. As you just saw, a heavier load reduces the average dc voltage level. The ability of a power supply to maintain a constant output voltage as line voltage or load current changes is known as *regulation*. Regulators stabilize a filtered dc signal to a smooth, constant level. Unregulated supplies are never used to power digital circuits. Ripple can cause unpredictable operation in even the most rugged integrated circuits, so you can expect to find a regulated supply in your printer. There are two methods of voltage regulation: linear and switching. Power supplies are usually classified in that way.

Linear regulation is just as the name implies—current flows continuously (or linearly) from the regulator's input to its output. Figures 5-8 and 5-9 illustrate two typical approaches to linear regulation.

While you could see many various applications of linear regulators, the principles are always the same. A regulator composed of discrete components (or the equivalent components fabricated onto an IC chip) is designed to output only a certain voltage as long as its input voltage exceeds some minimum level that is higher than the desired output. You can see this illustrated in the diagrams of Figs. 5-8 and 5-9. As long as filtered dc is sufficiently higher than the desired output, a regulator can supply a smooth dc voltage that remains constant over a wide variation of

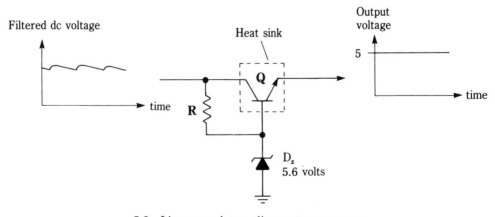

5-8 Linear regulator—discrete components.

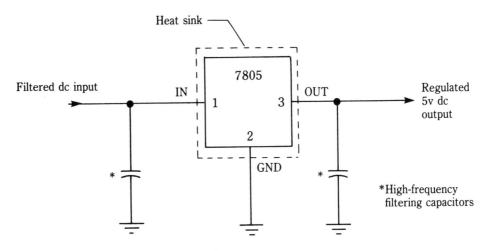

5-9 Linear regulator—IC.

load demands—the output is regulated. If the input voltage falls below its minimum level, then the supply falls out of regulation.

In order to maintain its constant output voltage, the regulating circuit (or IC) essentially "throws away" extra energy provided by the filter in the form of heat. This is why regulators are often attached to large metal heat sinks. Excess heat is carried away by ambient air. Figure 5-10 shows a complete linear-regulated power supply typical of what you might find in a printer. There could be more than one regulator to provide multiple output voltages.

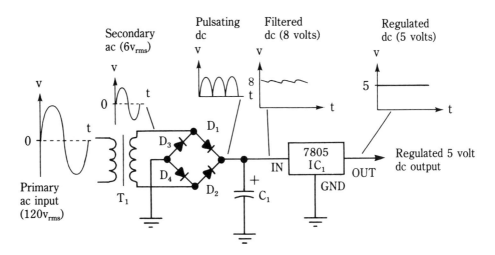

5-10 Linear-regulated power supply.

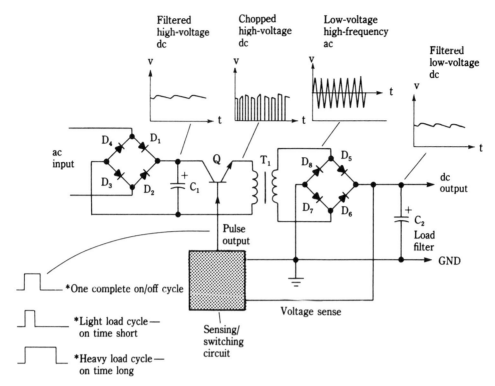

5-11   Switching-regulated power supply.

You might think that throwing away excess energy is a waste—and you are exactly right. Linear power supplies are only up to 50 percent efficient. This means that for every 10 watts of power delivered to the supply, only 5 watts ever reach the load. Much of this waste occurs in the regulation process. Switching-regulated power supplies offer more efficiency over linear-regulated designs.

Instead of throwing away extra energy like a linear regulator does, a switching regulator senses the output voltage level, then switches the ac primary (or secondary) voltage on and off as required to maintain a desired output voltage. Figure 5-11 shows this in more detail. Switching occurs at a very high rate, usually 20 to 40 kHz (cycles per second). Under light load conditions when little current is needed by the load, "on" time of a switching cycle is short. As load current demands increase, "on" time will also increase to supply more energy to the load. In this way, the power supply provides *only* as much power as its load requires—no more. If a load requires more power than a switching supply can provide, it will fall out of regulation just as a linear supply would.

Switching circuits can be rather complex, but their sole purpose is to sense voltage at the load, compare that voltage to a reference value, then generate a switching pulse of proportional duration and frequency to drive a switch. In most cases, the switching element is actually a high-power transistor located at either the primary or secondary side of a transformer.

Switching-regulated power supplies are popular because of their efficiency—many designs can exceed 85 percent efficiency. For every 10 watts of power delivered to the supply, 8.5 watts or more is available to the load. Less power is dissipated as heat, so supplies run cooler and use smaller components to convert the same amount of power. Switching supplies are common in printers.

In spite of their higher efficiency, the operating frequency of switching supplies can cause electrical noise interference in some circuits. Be sure to replace any metal coverings or noise shieldings that you remove from a switching power supply. You might also note that the load regulation of switching power supplies is not as good as equivalent linear supplies.

Power supply problems

Use extreme caution when troubleshooting any type of power supply! Ac voltage right from a wall outlet can be *lethal*. Before you continue with this chapter, review chapter 3 for a list of precautions and considerations when working with high voltages.

Whenever you are measuring ac voltages, remember that your multimeter is reading in root mean square (RMS) values. While the history and mathematical significance of RMS is beyond the scope of this book, you should realize that the ac voltage on your multimeter is less than its peak by a factor of 0.707. Figure 5-12 illustrates the relationship between peak and RMS readings. All ac meters average the peak values of ac signals to show RMS readings. If you wish to know the peak value of your RMS reading, simply multiply the RMS value by 1.414. For example, 10 volts RMS would equal $(10 \times 1.414 =)$ 14.14 volts peak.

Symptom The power supply is completely dead. No power indicators are lit and the printer does not function at all.

Before you go into this repair, take a moment to check some of the obvious things. Be sure the printer is actually plugged in and that its outlet is live. Inspect fuses inside the printer to find any that might have failed. If you are unable to

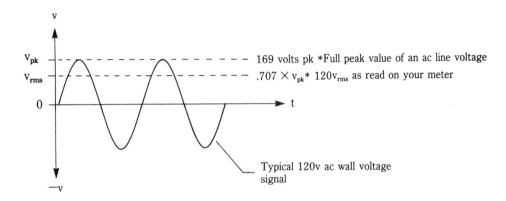

5-12 Comparison of peak and rms voltage values.

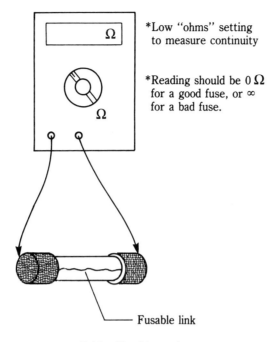

*Low "ohms" setting
to measure continuity

*Reading should be 0 Ω
for a good fuse, or ∞
for a bad fuse.

Fusable link

5-13 Checking a fuse.

decide if a fuse is good or bad just by looking at it, you can measure its continuity with your multimeter as shown in Fig. 5-13. Check for any transformer switch in the rear of your printer and be sure that it is in the 120 volt position (220 volt for European printers).

If there is any question about the presence of ac at the printer's wall outlet, measure the ac voltage at the wall receptacle as shown in Fig. 5-14. Set your multimeter to its highest ac voltage scale before taking your measurement. Use *extreme* caution when measuring ac at any electrical outlet. An operational ac outlet should read between 110 and 125 volts ac (RMS). If the line voltage is too low for any reason, your power supply might not be able to generate enough power to operate the printer.

When you are confident that adequate power is reaching the printer, it is time to begin measuring critical voltages in the supply itself. No repair is worth the cost of a personal injury, so *please* use caution whenever making measurements in a power supply. If your supply uses switching regulation, it is probably shrouded by metal shielding to reduce radio frequency (RF) emissions. Any shielding must be replaced correctly to ensure reliable operation of the printer.

Follow Procedure 5-1 to evaluate the output voltages of a power supply. Power must be on for this procedure, so remember to observe all safety precautions. As you examine the power supply, look over each component for signs of failure such as a burn, crack, or break. You might find that one or all voltage outputs are defective. Procedure 5-2 guides you through an examination of typical signal levels to determine the point at which signals are lost.

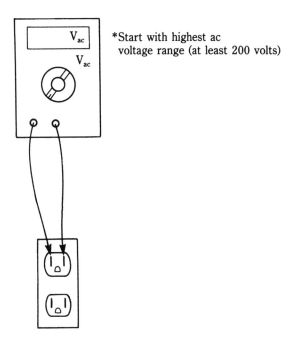

*Start with highest ac
voltage range (at least 200 volts)

5-14 Measuring voltage at an ac receptacle.

Symptom Power supply operation is intermittent.

Intermittent operation can be caused by several failures. Faulty wiring or an intermittent printed circuit connection can often result in erratic operation. Intermittent operation can also result from sudden physical shocks such as a drop. Procedure 5-3 provides details on searching out and repairing intermittent wiring.

If your printer works intermittently *only* after some period of use (5 minutes, 10 minutes, etc.), shutdown could be occurring due to excessive heat in the supply circuit. Many types of regulators (especially IC regulators) carry built-in overload and thermal shutdown protection. When heat builds up, the regulator(s) shut down until temperature returns to an acceptable level. A printer that seems to throw a good deal of heat might have poor ventilation. Examine any vents around the printer's housing and be sure they are all clear. If ventilation is clear, you might be faced with a marginal regulator.

Check the regulator for overheating by holding your palm at a safe distance over the device and letting heat convect upward. *Never* touch a component that you even suspect might be hot! An unusually hot regulator suggests a possible *thermal fault*. Try squirting a little liquid coolant (available from just about any electronics hobby store) on the suspect component. If operation promptly returns, you have isolated your fault. Replace the defective component.

Symptom The power indicator is lit, but the printer is not working (or not working properly).

This is often a much more subtle problem than those discussed so far. The entire printer relies upon adequate power from the supply. As you saw in chapter 4, print head problems can be rooted in a power supply failure. Logic and driver circuitry also require a source of constant power. If supply voltage fails or drops for any reason, symptoms can range from instances of erratic or missing print to a complete shutdown. Your own specific symptoms depend on your particular printer and the severity of the supply failure.

Start by exposing your supply. With power off, inspect any wiring leading off the supply (including connectors) to be certain that wiring is intact and connectors are seated properly as detailed in Procedure 5-3. Turn the printer on, then follow Procedure 5-1. Measure each output voltage at the power supply, and also at its termination in the electronic control package. If each output from the supply measures correctly, the defect probably lies in main logic or driver circuitry. See chapter 6 for explanations and troubleshooting techniques for electronic circuits. If you do find a defective voltage output, follow Procedure 5-2 to trace the defect into the supply circuit. When a power indicator light is lit, you will probably find adequate signal levels all the way to the filter. If you are unable to resolve a faulty output by replacing a regulator or other faulty device, replace the entire power supply.

Troubleshooting procedures

You will find that power supplies are not that difficult to troubleshoot. Linear-regulated supplies are very straightforward devices. Switching-regulated supplies can

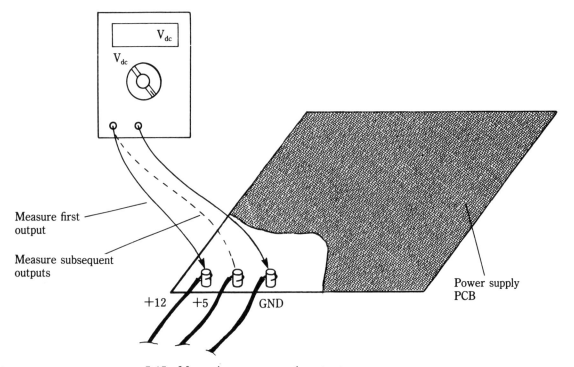

5-15   Measuring power supply outputs.

be much more complicated in terms of their component count, but the same symptoms are usually due to the same general causes.

⬤ **Procedure 5-1** Check power supply circuits.

Before you start changing components in a power supply, you must first determine whether the supply itself is defective or the fault exists elsewhere. A check of the supply output(s) provides a quick indication of the problem source. Attach the common probe of your multimeter to the supply ground terminal. It might be labeled "0v," "GND," "G," or "COM." Locate your first output terminal. Most power supplies label their outputs, so you should have little trouble determining the appropriate output values. Set your multimeter to its highest dc voltage range, then measure an output. Common voltage outputs include 5-, 12-, and 24-volts dc. This is illustrated in Fig. 5-15.

If your voltage measures several volts *above* what is expected, then the regulator might be internally short-circuited. In that event, filter voltage might be traveling straight through the regulator without control. A voltage *less* than expected can mean one of three things. First, the regulator's output can be shorting to ground, or a short circuit in the load is possibly dragging the output below its rated value. Zero volts at an output (with a normal filter voltage) suggests an open regulator. To further isolate your regulator, disconnect your supply from its load circuit and measure the supply output again. If normal output voltage returns, there could be a short in the load circuit(s) (logic, drivers, motors, etc.). Disconnecting a load might not work with switching-regulated supplies. They need some sort of load at all times to ensure stable voltage sensing and switching performance.

⬤ **Procedure 5-2** Check supply signals.

When you are faced with a faulty output, it is necessary to trace the signal path in order to determine just where the desired signals are being lost. Figure 5-16 shows a set of typical readings at key points in a conventional linear-regulated power supply designed to provide 12-volts dc. It makes little practical difference whether or not you start from the ac input and work toward the dc output, or vice

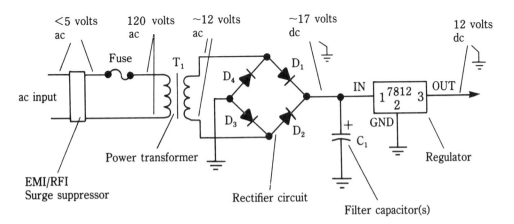

5-16 Typical ac and dc voltages in a 12 volt linear power supply.

versa. What *is* important is that you stay consistent—do not bounce back and forth around the supply or you could become lost. Since you started measurements at the regulator output in Procedure 5-1, it is a good idea to start from this point.

Measure the dc input voltage to the regulator. This is also the output voltage across the filter. It should be several volts higher than the expected output. If the regulator's input equals its output (but is above the expected output), the regulator could be shorted internally. Replace the regulator. If the input is less than the expected output voltage, the regulator might be ineffective since its input must exceed its output by several volts to operate properly. In the event of a low input voltage, turn the printer power off and check the filter capacitor(s) for internal shorts. Also check any diodes in the rectifier array for open circuits. Follow the appropriate troubleshooting guidelines of chapter 3 to test individual components. A failure in the filter or rectifier can easily reduce input voltage to a regulator. Replace any faulty component.

Measure the ac input voltage to the rectifier. It should read about the same value as (or higher than) the expected dc output. This is the secondary voltage across the transformer. Also measure the ac primary voltage. Most power transformers are marked with appropriate voltage levels on the outer housing or wrappings. Check that your readings approximate the transformer's markings. If the primary voltage is correct and the secondary voltage is low, there might be a short within the secondary winding itself. An unusually hot transformer is another indication of a possible internal short. Replace the faulty transformer. If primary voltage reads low, inspect the wiring between the ac cord and the transformer primary. There might be a noise filter/surge protector device in the line. A failure here could reduce primary voltage, as well as carry through to the rest of the supply. Measure ac voltage entering and leaving the noise filter (is used). Ideally, there should be a difference of less than 5-volts ac. A more significant difference suggests a faulty device. Replace the noise filter or surge protector.

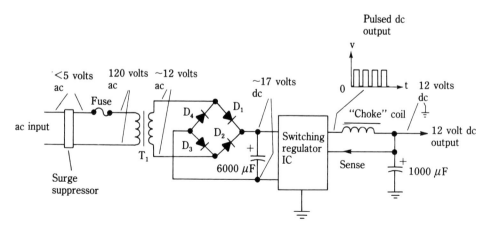

5-17   Typical ac and dc voltages in a 12 volt switching power supply—IC switching regulator.

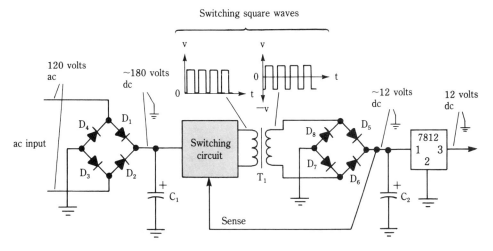

5-18   Typical ac and dc voltages in a 12 volt switching power supply—discrete switching regulator.

Switching power supplies can be approached in a similar fashion, but you should expect to find different readings as suggested by Figs. 5-17 and 5-18. Sensing and switching in Fig. 5-17 is provided by a single integrated circuit switching regulator, which can provide one or more outputs. The actual output of the IC is a high-frequency high-voltage (higher than the expected dc output) square wave signal. The IC senses load voltage and current demands, then continuously adjusts the duty cycle of the square wave (on time versus off time) to supply enough energy to the load filter to hold a desired output.

Supplies that use discrete switching circuits as shown in Fig. 5-18 will offer slightly different readings. Note that the circuit is actually two power supplies. An input side of the supply rectifies and filters a 120-volt ac signal to produce a high-voltage dc level at the switching network. The switching network itself is composed of discrete transistors that sense voltage output and alter the duty cycle of each switching pulse.

A power transformer is used after the switching circuit to step down high-voltage pulses to a normal level that can be rerectified, refiltered, and regulated to a load circuit. Due to the high-frequency nature of switch pulses, your multimeter is unable to acquire meaningful information in the transformer area. If you have access to an oscilloscope, however, you can probe deeper into the switching circuit by observing high-frequency pulses. They should appear similar to those shown in Figs. 5-17 and 5-18.

● **Procedure 5-3**   Check the wiring and circuit board.

Wiring problems, either in cabling or in printed circuit traces, can yield some of the most deceptive and frustrating problems found in power supplies (or any other electrical circuit). Power supply circuit boards with their relatively large, heavy components are prime candidates for stress fractures and solder joint failures.

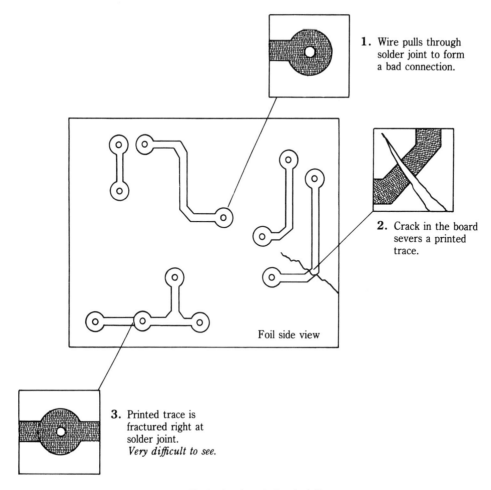

1. Wire pulls through solder joint to form a bad connection.

2. Crack in the board severs a printed trace.

Foil side view

3. Printed trace is fractured right at solder joint. *Very difficult to see.*

5-19 Typical printed circuit failures.

Keep in mind printed circuit boards do not crack spontaneously. If the printer is dropped or abused, the physical shock could apply enough force to crack the board as shown in Fig. 5-19. Three typical failure modes are illustrated: a solder failure, a printed wiring break, and a board break. These types of problems can appear *anywhere*, not just in the places shown in Fig. 5-19.

Soldering, when performed correctly, forms a strong electromechanical bond between a wire and printed circuit trace. While solder joints are typically strong, they are not indestructible. Inspect the printed circuit board with all power disconnected. If you find a component lead wrenched from its joint, simply resolder it carefully. Bad solder joints such as this are usually easy to spot.

Cracks in the board are also reasonably obvious. When a crack travels across a printed trace, it often splits the trace as well. The most reliable way to repair such a crack is to solder a jumper wire between both *ends* of the trace. Do *not* try to jump a crack with a solder bridge. Solder does not adhere well to the coatings used on circuit boards, so chances are your bridge will not hold up over time.

A more evasive split can occur where a trace reaches its solder pad. These types of breaks are difficult to see because they are hidden by the solder joint. You can check for broken traces by gently wiggling the solder pads of suspect connections. They should not move when wiggled. If a pad moves and its trace does not, you can see any break in the trace there. As with a printed circuit crack, you can correct the problem by soldering a jumper wire between both *ends* of the trace.

Chapter 6

Electronics

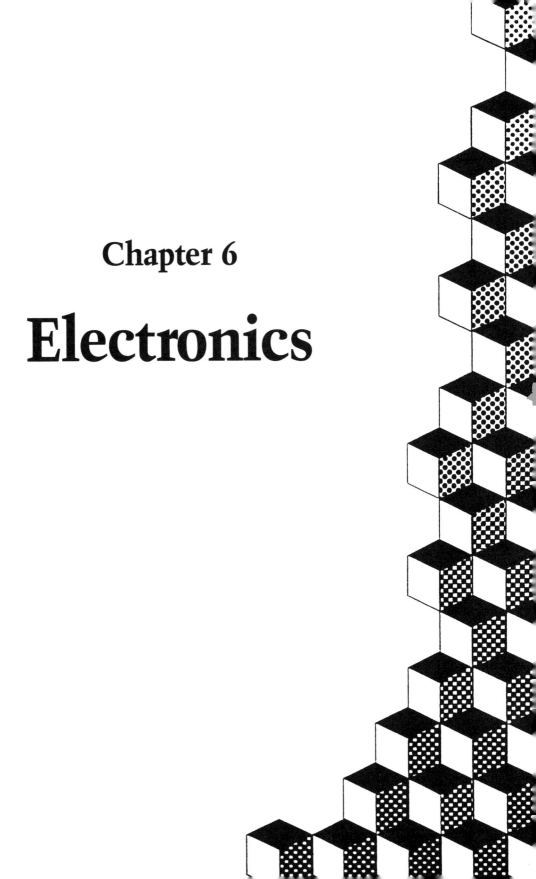

Each and every operation in your printer, regardless of its technology, is driven by electronic circuitry. While the individual components and their complexity can vary greatly depending on the technology used and your particular printer model, all printer circuitry must perform essentially the same operations. This universality makes it easier for you to understand what is going on in your printer, no matter what type of printer it is. In this chapter, you learn about the components and operations of a generic electronics control package, as well as steps you can take to troubleshoot and repair some simple failures.

How the electronics works

Printer electronics must be capable of performing several important tasks. First, it must communicate with the outside world. This involves not only the host computer, but the user as well. It must drive one or more motors—one for paper feed and one for carriage transport (or one for drum rotation in the case of an electrostatic printer). It must interpret sensor information such as "out of paper" or "head overheating," along with a continuous monitoring of the print head's position. It must translate communicated data, usually in ASCII format, into dot patterns that its print head can deliver, then drive the print head to produce those patterns. Finally, all of these functions must be coordinated to work together. As you read in chapter 2, all of these tasks are performed by the *electronic control package* (ECP).

Figure 6-1 shows a block diagram of a basic ECP. It is composed of five major sections: an interface circuit, a data buffer, a control panel, a driver circuit, and main logic.

The *interface circuit* handles data communication between computer and printer. Either a *serial* or *parallel* interface could be used and sometimes both are available. Both types manage the flow of information and control signals into and out of the printer. Data entering the printer is temporarily stored in a *data buffer* consisting of Random Access Memory (RAM) array until it can be processed.

Communication between printer and user is accomplished through a *control panel* usually positioned somewhere on the top or front of the printer. Most printers allow you to select operating parameters such as font style or character pitch through combinations of keyboard controls.

High-energy electromechanical devices like motors or solenoids are controlled by power components contained in a *driver circuit*. The driver circuit also generates any signals necessary for operating the print head. Sensor signals generally travel through the driver system where they are interpreted.

All operations are coordinated and tied together by a *main logic* circuit. This contains the central processing unit (CPU) and a permanent program memory that defines dot patterns for each printed character, and tells the printer how to perform

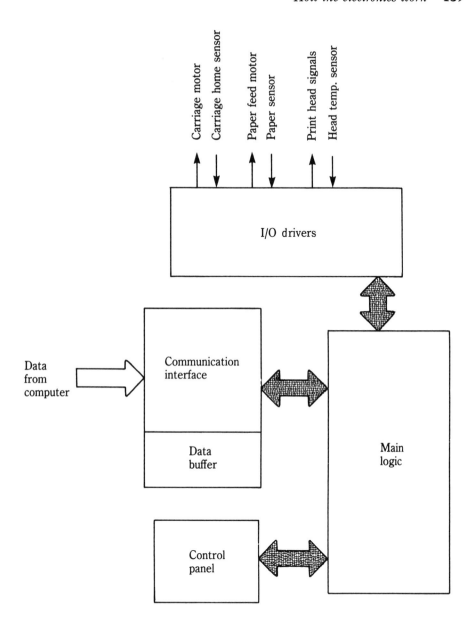

6-1 Block diagram of an electronics control package.

basic functions like carriage positioning, paper advance, or other operating information.

Although this might sound like an extensive amount of circuitry, the parts and components necessary to operate a typical commercial printer can often be built into one or two printed circuit boards as shown in Fig. 6-2. The next section of this chapter familiarizes you with various types of integrated circuits and how they operate.

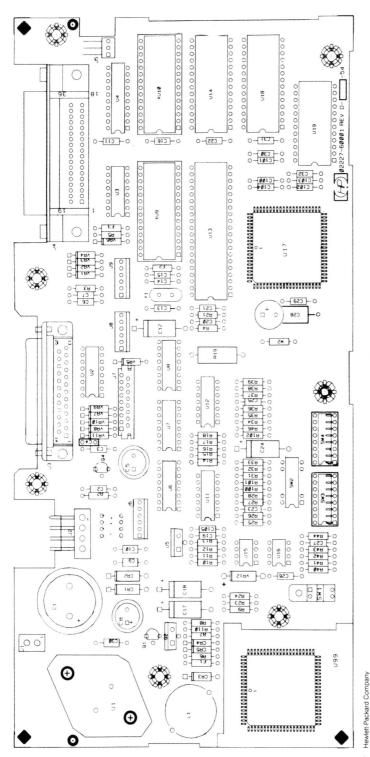

6-2 Board diagram of a printer circuit.

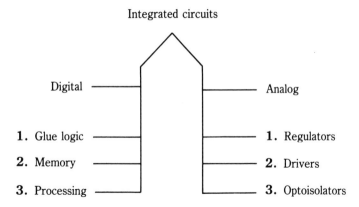

Integrated circuits

Digital — — Analog

1. Glue logic — — 1. Regulators

2. Memory — — 2. Drivers

3. Processing — — 3. Optoisolators

6-3 Common ICs found in printer circuits.

Electronic components

Chapter 3 introduced you to the wide variety of electronic components you can encounter in ordinary printer circuits. This section expands that discussion with a detailed review of typical integrated circuits. Figure 6-3 illustrates the breakdown of ICs that you might see. Analog ICs generally interact with the outside world through such devices as drivers, regulators, and optoisolators. Digital ICs often make up the majority of components as memory devices, processing components, or "glue logic" used to interconnect signals from other digital ICs. Figure 6-3 by no means represents every possible type of IC you could encounter in the electronics field, but most printer ICs fall into these categories.

Digital integrated circuits

Most of the operations performed in your printer are digital. Information and instructions are processed in terms of binary levels—on or off, true or false. Ideally, a binary 1 is equal to +5-volts dc, and a binary 0 is equal to 0-volts dc. In reality, you can expect a binary 1 to range anywhere from +3.2 volts to about +4.8 volts, while a binary 0 will stay below +0.8 volts.

Glue logic devices (also known as *discrete logic*) are the building blocks of all digital systems. They offer basic Boolean logic operations as shown in Fig. 6-4. You can easily substitute voltage levels for logic conditions to determine what voltage should exist at the inputs and output for each logic combination. There could be anywhere from one to six glue logic gates packaged onto one IC chip.

Frequently, you can identify glue logic components by the prefix of their part numbers. Part numbers beginning with *74*, such as 7408 or 74,128, belong to the Transistor-Transistor Logic (TTL) family. Parts with a *40* prefix, such as 4016 or 4032, are in the complementary metal oxide semiconductors (CMOS) family. Although there are important differences in the fabrication and electrical characteristics of these two families, Boolean logic operations are the same for both. A

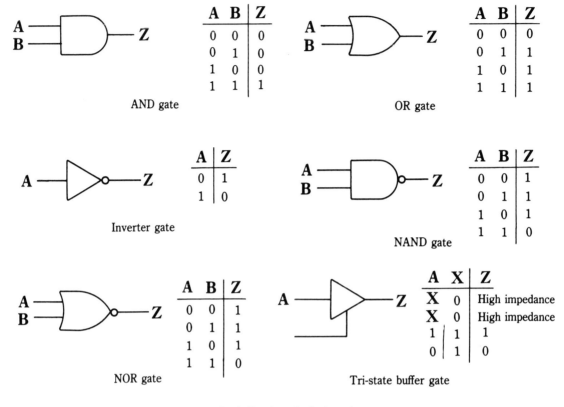

6-4 Basic Boolean logic functions.

manufacturer's data book can help you identify the specific part, as well as what each IC pin does. You can see two examples in Fig. 6-5. Remember there are many other functions available in these glue logic families besides just Boolean logic operations. One-shots, flip-flops, shift registers, and decoders are only some of the other functions you will find.

Discrete logic ICs are rarely of much use by themselves. Older printers combine individual logic functions to handle the complex operations that are required. With the advent of very large scale integration (VLSI) components (e.g., microprocessors), much of the discrete logic has been replaced by fewer, more powerful devices. This makes the job of troubleshooting easier. Glue logic, however, is still widely used to tie together the operations of these complex devices.

Memory circuits are used to hold data and program instructions. The most notable use of memory is found in the printer's data buffer. ASCII characters traveling over the communications interface have to be stored temporarily until they can be handled by the central processor. Since this memory is only intended to be temporary, RAM components are used. When power is removed, any data in RAM is lost. A typical data buffer can range from several thousand bytes (kilobytes) in simple moving-head printers, to several million bytes (megabytes) for electrostatic printers.

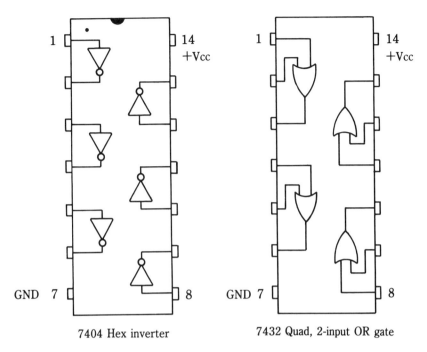

7404 Hex inverter   7432 Quad, 2-input OR gate

6-5   Typical glue logic components.

A more subtle use of RAM is "scratchpad memory" for the microprocessor. The CPU must store computations and variables as the printer operates. It might not need much more than 100 bytes or so, but it is critically important to the microprocessor. A scratchpad memory can also hold operator parameters set from the control panel (e.g., font style or character pitch).

Since essentially all printers today run under microprocessor control, there must be a permanent source of instructions and commands to manage the conversion of ASCII characters into dot patterns, respond to sensor signals, or act on control panel inputs. This information does not come from the computer, which only sends out characters for printing. This internal source of instruction, or *program*, is fixed, so it never varies. As a result, it might be stored on a read only memory (ROM) device. When power is turned off, ROM data remains intact. Printers that are more complex or contain more features usually hold a larger amount of ROM.

Regardless of whether memory is temporary or permanent, a memory IC has three sets of signals as shown in Fig. 6-6: address signals, data signals, and control signals. The *address* specifies a precise location where data is to be read or stored. Remember data can only be read from ROM devices. *Control* signals select an individual memory device and specify a read or write operation. *Data* signals are then written to or from the specified address location, and a new address can be selected.

Microprocessors are complex, programmable logic circuits that can produce one or more digital outputs based on digital input data (instructions or variables).

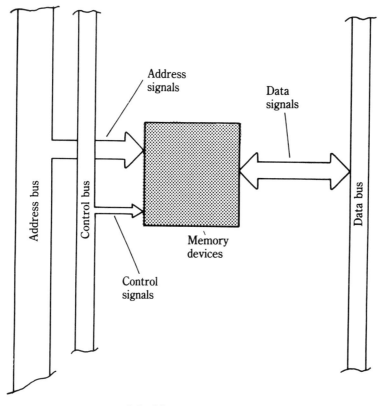

6-6 Memory structure.

A program contained in ROM instructs the microprocessor in its decision-making process. It is the microprocessor that translates ASCII words in the data buffer into dot patterns based upon the selected font style, pitch, and enhancements, then delivers those dot patterns to the print head driver. The microprocessor also detects and handles conditions like "paper out" or "head overheat," and reports those errors back to the computer through the interface. It also controls paper advance and carriage motion. Whenever a new font style or printing process must be changed, a new program ROM (or ROMs) can be installed, alleviating the need for a circuit re-design. It is this type of flexibility that makes current printers so powerful.

While the microprocessors typically found in printers are simpler than those used in computers, they all carry the same general signals as shown in Fig. 6-7. Address locations are generated by the microprocessor to specify every possible piece of data or instruction that is used. Data can be read or written over the data lines. In some cases, the microprocessor writes out a command or data word. In other cases, it reads data or instructions existing on the data lines. Control signals might enter the microprocessor to inform it of conditions in the printer, or leave it to control memory and interface operations.

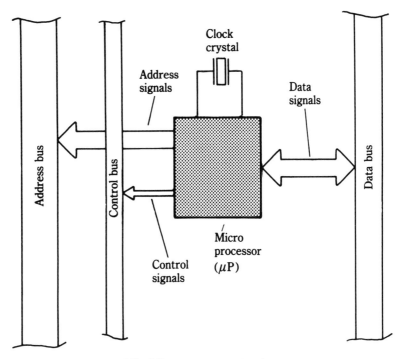

6-7 Microprocessor structure.

Your printer might also carry an application-specific integrated circuit (ASIC) to augment the microprocessor's speed and functions. An ASIC is essentially a custom IC designed exclusively for use in your particular printer. It will often form a bridge between the microprocessor and the drivers, control panel, and communications interface. When an ASIC is used, it is usually the device that provides dot patterns and motor signals to their respective drivers, as well as coordinates operation of the communication interface. This frees valuable processing time for the microprocessor. It also eliminates a tremendous amount of glue logic that would otherwise be needed to isolate the microprocessor from the demands of the outside world. You can easily identify an ASIC as a square IC located close to the microprocessor. An older ASIC might be packaged as a large DIP, but it will still be close to its microprocessor.

Analog integrated circuits

In spite of the speed and processing power offered by digital circuits, few digital components are capable of supplying the current and voltage demands of real-world devices such as motors and solenoids. Some types of external sensors do not lend themselves readily to digital interpretation. To overcome these limitations, analog ICs are often employed to condition digital signals for the outside world, or vice versa. You normally find three types of analog ICs: regulators, drivers, and optoisolators.

Table 6-1. Linear regulator families

7800 family		7900 family	
Device	Output (V_{dc})	Device	Output (V_{dc})
7805	5 V	7905	−5 V
7806	6 V	7906	−6 V
7808	8 V	7908	−8 V
7810	10 V	7909	−9 V
7812	12 V	7912	−12 V
7815	15 V	7915	−15 V
7818	18 V	7918	−18 V
7824	24 V	7924	−24 V

You learned about regulators in chapter 5. They are used to control the voltage levels generated by a power supply. There are two basic families of linear regulator that you can identify directly from their part number. The 7800 family is a group of positive voltage regulators whose output voltage is specified by the last two digits in the part number. For example, a 7805 is a +5-volt regulator, a 7815 is a +15-volt regulator, and so on. The 7900 family is a group of negative voltage regulators whose negative output is also specified by the last two part number digits. A 7910 would be a −10-volt regulator. Table 6-1 lists the common devices that you might find in the 7800 and 7900 families. Each of these regulators is a three-terminal device manufactured in a TO-220 case.

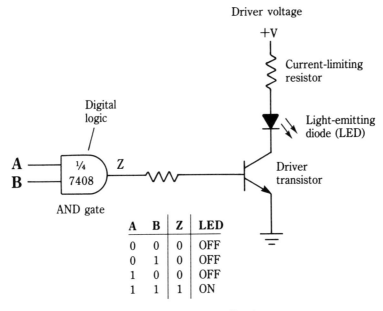

6-8 Simple driver application.

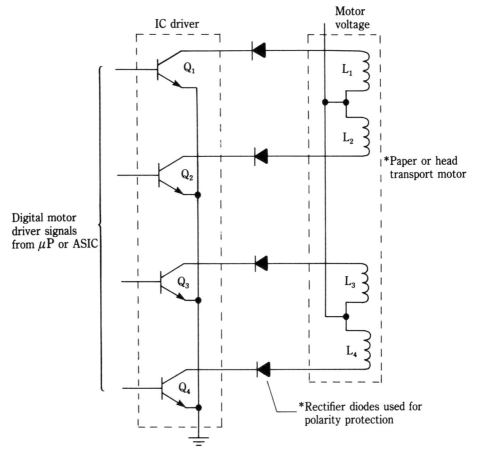

6-9 Typical IC driver.

A *driver* is simply an amplifier. It is used to translate low-power digital signals into signals with appropriate voltage and current levels to operate high-power devices. Figure 6-8 demonstrates this principle with a basic circuit that drives a light-emitting diode with a conventional TTL AND gate. By itself, the TTL gate could not supply enough power to light the LED properly without destroying itself. Some type of amplifier is needed to interface the gate and the LED. A transistor driver is inserted into the circuit which handles the higher voltage and current under control of the AND gate.

For low-to-moderate power needs, several drive elements can be fabricated onto a single IC as shown in Fig. 6-9. When applications require substantial amounts of power, however, discrete transistors can be used. IC drivers might be difficult to identify on sight since there are no "typical" families of part numbers. You should refer to a manufacturer's data or cross-reference book for specific information. Figure 6-10 illustrates a 10-pin single in-line package (SIP) STA403A quad driver. Some drivers are also available in regular DIP configurations.

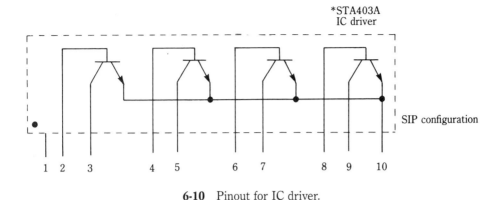

6-10   Pinout for IC driver.

Optical isolation is another means used to connect real-world signals with electronic circuits. Optoisolators are self-contained components that provide a built-in optical emitter and detector as shown in Fig. 6-11. A signal from the outside world such as a carriage home or paper out condition is applied to the emitter. In most cases, the emitter is a visible or infrared LED. When a signal is applied, the LED turns on. Light traverses an open gap from the LED to stimulate the base lead of a phototransistor. Light turns on the phototransistor, so it effectively detects the presence of a real-world signal. The detector circuit can then condition the signal and provide it to the main logic for a response.

The tremendous advantage of optoisolators is that they can connect signals from one circuit to another without any physical wiring connections at all. This principle is illustrated in Fig. 6-12. Suppose Circuit A is a sensor board detecting the presence of paper, and generates a +12-volt signal when paper is in place. Unfortunately, +12 volts will damage TTL logic. An optoisolator carries the signal without transferring any voltage, so an appropriate TTL signal can be developed in Circuit B from the detector's output.

Another advantage of optical isolation is circuit protection. In the example of Fig. 6-12, if a failure should occur in either circuit, optical isolation prevents electronic damage from spreading to associated circuits. Only signals will be absent.

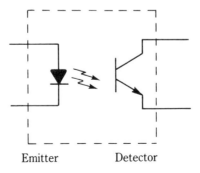

Emitter   Detector

6-11   Typical optoisolator.

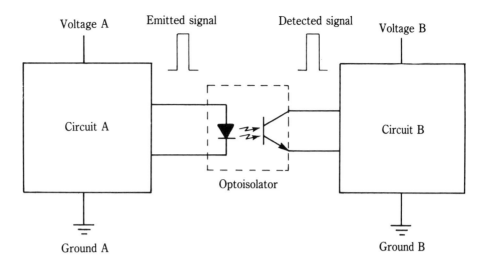

6-12 Circuit isolation using optoisolators.

Optoisolator part numbers are almost impossible to discern on sight, but you can usually identify them based on their case styles as shown in Fig. 6-13. Older devices were packaged as cylinders, while many current versions are packaged as 4- or 6-pin DIPs.

Main logic

The main logic forms the core of the electronic control package. As Fig. 6-14 and 6-15 illustrate, main logic is composed of the microprocessor, ASIC (if present), memory devices (ROM and RAM), and any glue logic devices such as gates or buffers needed to tie logic operations together. Figure 6-14 shows a typical configuration with an ASIC installed, while Fig. 6-15 shows a similar circuit without an ASIC. Notice that where ASIC is omitted, a secondary (or "slave") microprocessor or extensive glue logic is needed to remove some of the processing burden from the main microprocessor. Remember the thick lines in these figures represent *busses* (groups of signal wires) and not just a single wire.

When power is first turned on, main logic performs a "cold start" initialization. It seeks instructions from the program ROM that will guide the printer through a RAM check, send the print head to its "home" position, and establish communications with the host computer (if connected). Your particular printer might perform its initialization slightly differently. Electrostatic printers often take several minutes to initialize, since fusing rollers must warm to some minimum temperature. There is also much more RAM to test than for a normal moving-head printer. If trouble should occur in the main logic, it often manifests itself during initialization.

Microprocessor and digital logic troubleshooting is an involved, and often difficult process—especially for the novice. Before disassembling your printer, be sure

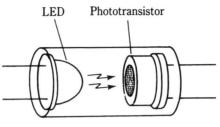

Cylindrical package

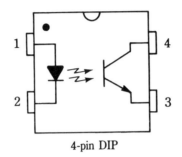

4-pin DIP

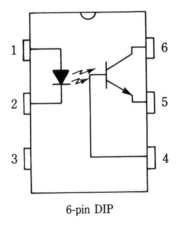

6-pin DIP

6-13 Optoisolator packages.

the failure is not caused by your host computer. Some printers might not initialize if they are not connected to the computer. Try your printer on a different computer, or try a working printer on your computer. Perhaps a friend or colleague might consider loaning you their printer for a brief check. (In troubleshooting, this is known as a "sanity check.") If your printer functions properly on another computer, and another working printer fails to function on your computer, then suspect a problem in your computer's communications interface, software package, or cable.

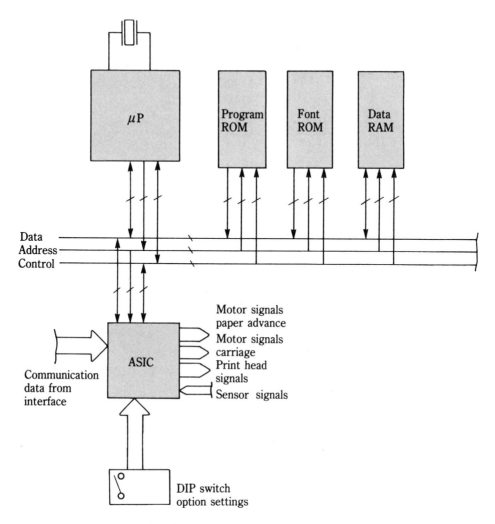

6-14   Main logic diagram—with an ASIC.

You might have to alter some communications variables on your printer (especially with serial interfaces) so that it should work on someone else's computer, and vice versa. However, if your printer continues to fail on another system and a working printer operates properly on your computer, you have isolated the trouble to your printer. Go ahead with the repair procedures in this chapter.

It also helps to have a set of schematics on hand as well to indicate the location and operation of the printers components. You could contact the printer's manufacturer directly, or second-source your documentation from Howard W. Sams & Co. They offer excellent documentation packages for older printers. Their address and phone number are listed in appendix D.

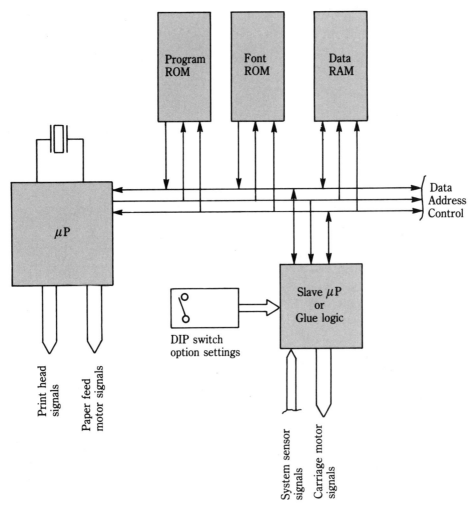

6-15   Main logic diagram—without an ASIC.

Troubleshooting main logic

Symptom   The printer's power indicator is lit, but it fails to initialize. There is no apparent activity in the printer after power is turned on. The self-test mode does not work.

This immediately suggests that your printer is not initializing properly, if at all. The control panel probably does not respond, and its self-test mode will not work. You should suspect a failure somewhere in the main logic elements of your electronics. There are several possible circumstances that can cause these symptoms.

Start by checking the system clock as explained in Procedure 6-1. Although the microprocessor wields the processing power in your printer, it cannot operate without timing signals provided by a clock oscillator. Most microprocessors have an oscillator built onto their IC chips, but a piezoelectric crystal and frequency stabilizing capacitors are needed externally to fix the clock rate. Figure 6-2 shows the relationship of the crystal (Y1) to a microprocessor (XU9). The crystal is always as close as possible to the microprocessor.

A memory failure can sometimes cause the initialization process to freeze. RAM is tested each time the printer is powered up by writing a known value to each RAM location, then reading the stored value back again. If the known and stored values match, that memory location is assumed to be correct. If they do not, a memory failure is possible. Procedure 6-2 offers a general procedure that might give you a ballpark idea of memory integrity. Some printers stop immediately upon a defective memory location, while others allow the process to finish, but *no* printer will operate with a memory problem.

The microprocessor or ASIC could be faulty. Procedure 6-3 guides you through a series of measurements that might indicate the state of your processing components. Since every program instruction (including initialization instructions) is channeled through the microprocessor, a defect prevents any processing operations at all.

Symptom The printer appears to initialize, but it does not print under computer control. Self-test checks correctly.

A self-test pattern is a test of the printer's text and graphic capability. It can be initiated from a combination of control panel keystrokes. The program that drives the self-test sequence is contained in ROM and processed by the microprocessor (and ASIC). When a self-test works properly, it suggests that ROM, RAM and processing components are functional.

Another advantage of the printer's self-test is that other portions of the printer (carriage, print head, motors, etc.) are also tested—they would have to be functional in order to form a clear test pattern. If the printer appears to initialize, but will not print as directed by a computer, you should suspect a defect in the printer's communication interface. Data from the computer is not reaching the data buffer. Follow Procedure 6-4 to examine your communication interface circuits.

Symptom The printer initializes, but it does not print. The "paper out" indicator is lit even though paper is threaded.

Check your sensors! A printer stops its operation whenever it detects such an error. The paper sensor (either an optoisolator or a mechanical switch) detects the presence of paper when threaded properly. An enable signal from the sensor is interpreted by the main logic. If this sensor is faulty (or paper is threaded incorrectly), the printer may be fooled into "thinking" that there is no paper. Procedure 6-5 shows you how to test your sensors.

Symptom The printer prints, but its print is garbled or erratic. The self-test checks properly.

Before you tear your printer apart, be sure that any communication cable between your computer and printer is tightly connected. Also check your computer's software to see that it drives the printer correctly.

A printer that works in its self-test mode but produces garbled or erratic print under computer control might be suffering from a failing communications interface. Not all data is entering the data buffer, or data is being lost somewhere in the printer's electronics. Use Procedure 6-4 to test the communications circuit.

If the self-test proves to be erratic, the trouble could be in the power supply. Your logic voltage level might be marginal or intermittent. Refer to chapter 5 for background and troubleshooting information on power supplies.

I/O drivers

Drivers typically operate with three sets of signals in a printer: print head signals, carriage motor signals, and paper advance motor signals. As you saw earlier in this chapter, drivers are little more than simple amplifiers that translate low-power digital signals into high-power signals that can drive real-world devices. Figure 6-16 illustrates a general driver application using discrete transistors to fire print wires in an impact dot-matrix print head.

Optoisolators can also be considered driver devices. Their ability to couple signals without electrical connection makes them ideal for position sensing (along with microswitches). An important use for optoisolators is in tracking the speed and direction of a carriage. Figure 6-17 shows the basic principles of head position encoding.

A carriage motor is operated by voltage pulses. Each pulse represents a known linear distance across the page, so to place the carriage at a desired location, you only need to step some number of pulses left or right. The position encoder ensures that the carriage actually moves the right number of steps in the desired direction.

A code disk is nothing more than a small circle of clear plastic with opaque lines in it as shown on the left in Fig. 6-17. The disk is mounted between two

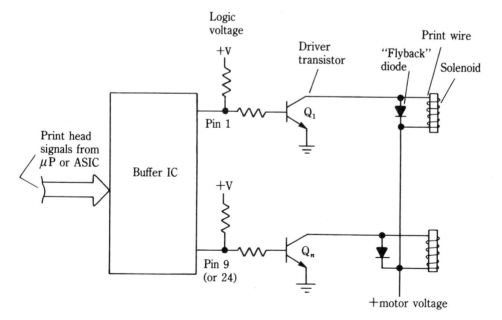

6-16   Discrete print head driver.

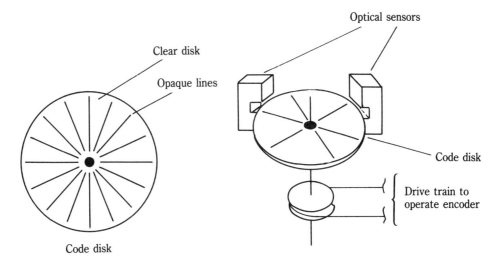

6-17 Optical encoding technique.

optoisolators and connected to the carriage motor. As the carriage moves, the code disk spins between both sensors, as shown on the right in Fig. 6-17. The disk's alternating clear and opaque lines turn each sensor on and off at high speed. This creates a chain of pulses from each sensor. Sensors are placed so that both pulse trains occur at slightly different times. This order (or *phase relationship*) will reverse as motor direction reverses.

Main logic counts these pulses. It also checks the phase of both pulse trains to ensure that movement is taking place in the desired direction. If the pulse count equals the original number of step pulses, the printer assumes that the carriage has reached its desired position. If not, additional pulses can be sent to correct the error.

Troubleshooting I/O drivers

Symptom The printer prints as expected, but one or more white (missing) or black lines are running through the print.

You could recognize these symptoms from various print-head symptoms of chapter 4. Impact, ink jet, and thermal print heads can suffer from these symptoms to some degree. Barring a failure in the print head itself, the next likely location for trouble is in the driver circuits. Procedure 6-6 outlines the steps you can use to track down a driver problem.

Consider the diagram of Fig. 6-16. Although this suggests an impact dot-matrix print head, you could mentally substitute a thermal or ink jet head. Suppose the driver transistor at pin 1 was open-circuited. Current would never be switched through the solenoid, so it would never fire. This would leave an absence of dots from that pin which would appear as a white line. If the same driver were shorted to ground, current would flow continuously, so the solenoid would always be on. A black line would appear in the print. This is also true for thermal and ink jet devices.

Symptom   The carriage or paper advance does not appear to operate. This symptom persists during a self-test.

Inspect your mechanical linkages and connections carefully before spending time troubleshooting driver electronics. It is possible that a belt could be loose or broken, or a gear might have stripped or disengaged. Check for any foreign matter that might cause a mechanical jam. Chapter 7 explains the components and operations of your printer's motors and mechanical systems.

After you have eliminated any possibility of mechanical trouble, follow Procedure 6-6 to troubleshoot your driver circuits. Refer to Fig. 6-9 for a detailed illustration. Motors are multiphase devices. This means that a motor must be driven with an appropriate sequence of pulses with enough energy to actuate the motor. If one or more of the driver elements is defective (either open or shorted), the motor might not turn properly, if at all.

Finally, check your power supply as outlined in the procedures of chapter 5. A faulty power supply output might not provide enough energy to run a high-current device like a motor. The motor itself could be faulty. As motors grow old, heat generated through periods of prolonged use can break down the insulating enamel in a motor's windings. Eventually, this can result in a short circuit. Chapter 7 provides more information on motors and their testing.

Symptom   The printer prints, but its carriage positions erratically or incorrectly. This persists during a self-test.

If the position encoder should fail, the printer would be "blind" to its carriage location. While this might not stop the printer, it can result in garbled or erratic printing. Character spacing could be totally unpredictable. The encoder's code disk might simply be dirty or dusty, but one or both sensors might have failed. Follow Procedure 6-5 to examine your sensors.

The carriage motor might be jammed or failing. Any belts or linkages connecting the motor and carriage might be loose. See chapter 7 for motor and mechanical troubleshooting details.

Communication circuits

Printer communication is the transfer of ASCII characters and control codes (in the form of binary digits) between a computer and a printer. Communication can take place in parallel or serial format. Serial communication is a bidirectional link that transfers data and control codes one bit at a time over just a few wires. Handshaking can be accomplished either by codes sent over the link, or by discrete signals sent by separate wires. Parallel communication is a unidirectional link that transfers data and control codes as a whole word at a time over many wires. Handshaking is always provided through discrete signal wires. Both formats offer advantages and disadvantages, as you learned in chapter 2, and they are both in wide use today.

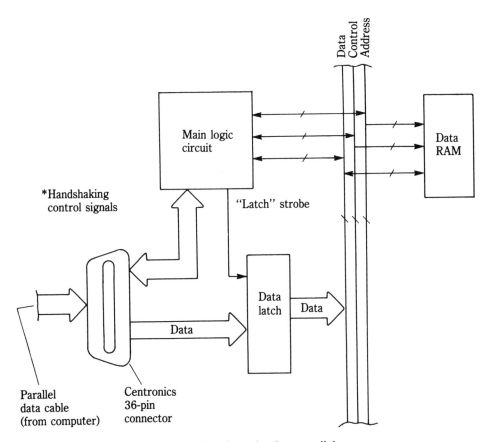

6-18　Interface circuits—parallel.

Block diagrams for basic parallel and serial interfaces are shown in Figs. 6-18 and 6-19. The parallel interface in Fig. 6-18 is heavily dependent on the microprocessor (or ASIC) to read data words latched onto a buffer port. A latch is used to retain the word until it can be stored in RAM. Main logic continues to read and store data until the RAM buffer is full, then main logic processes that information to run motors and the print head assembly. When the buffer is empty again, more requests for information are made to the computer, while RAM is refilled. Main logic generates any handshaking signals that are returned from the printer.

The serial interface shown in Fig. 6-19 is also dependent on main logic to store and process information, but it is complicated by the presence of a UART (or "interface chip") that converts serial bits to parallel words, and vice versa. Beyond the interface chip, data can be processed and printed exactly the same way as a parallel printer. Since many circumstances and symptoms involving communication problems have already been discussed in the section on main logic, they are not repeated here.

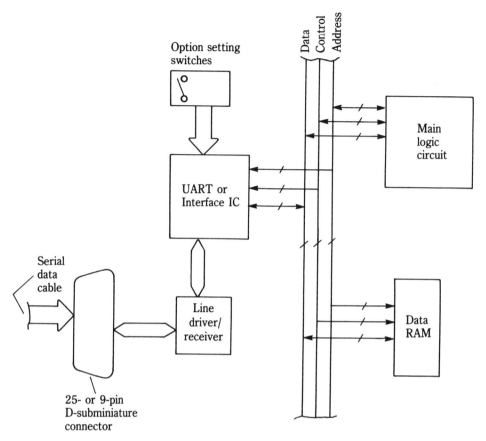

6-19   Interface circuits—serial.

Troubleshooting procedures

Dense electronic circuits such as your printer's electronic control package offer some unique difficulties that simpler circuits avoid. Timing and data signals vary at a high rate—so high that your multimeter will not be able to "see" them. For digital and microprocessor troubleshooting, you should use a good-quality logic probe that can detect high-frequency pulses as well as just binary 1s or 0s, and can switch between TTL and CMOS logic levels. Remember your printer circuitry might use a mixture of these ICs (but one family usually dominates). If you have access to an oscilloscope and can use it properly, it will be even more beneficial to you for digital testing.

Using a logic probe is not difficult. Attach the probe's "common" lead to a ground point on the printed circuit board (any ground point will do). This places the probe and circuit-under-test at the same reference point. Some probes are battery-powered, but others draw their power from the circuit. If you own an externally-powered probe, you must also attach the probe's power lead to a suitable logic voltage source in the circuit. With power and ground connected, simply touch

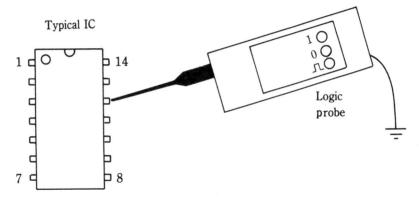

6-20 Measuring logic levels.

the probe's metal tip to any points you wish to measure, then read the logic conditions directly.

A properly connected logic probe is able to measure three things: logic highs (binary 1s), logic lows (binary 0s), and pulses (clocking or changing data levels). The appropriate conditions are indicated as lit LEDs on the probe. For most of the following test procedures, you will be concerned with clock and data signals. Figure 6-20 illustrates the use of a typical logic probe.

Beware of static discharge whenever you touch or handle an electronic circuit.

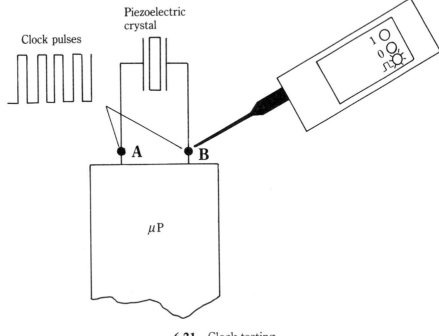

6-21 Clock testing.

Many ICs, especially sophisticated ICs like memories or microprocessors, are particularly sensitive to static electric charges. When you handle ICs or printed circuits, static buildup in your body can jump into an IC and destroy it internally. This can cause even more problems for your printer. Use a conductive wriststrap if it is possible. They are available from most electronic hobby stores. These straps essentially connect your skin to earth ground so that any static charges are taken away instead of building up in your body.

● **Procedure 6-1**   Check the printer's system clock.

A proper clock signal is crucial to the timing and operation of a microprocessor. If the clock fails for any reason, the processing components cease to function. The system clock is generated by an oscillator circuit built into the microprocessor, but an external piezoelectric crystal fixes the desired frequency.

Figure 6-21 shows a basic logic probe test of the system clock. Some printers run at 10 MHz or higher, so be sure your logic probe can detect pulses at that rate. Measure points "A" and "B" in turn. It might be necessary to follow the circuit traces a bit to find where the crystal and microprocessor connect. You should read a strong clock signal. If you detect a steady 1 or 0, the clock might not be working. Try replacing the piezoelectric crystal and check any supporting components (usually small value capacitors) that are stabilizing the crystal. If the clock still seems faulty, try replacing the microprocessor.

● **Procedure 6-2**   Check the printer's memory.

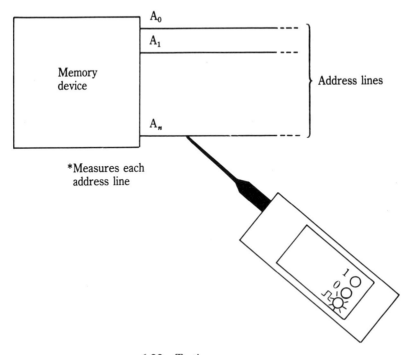

6-22   Testing memory.

A printer cannot work without a functioning memory to hold data from the computer. A failed memory component can precipitate a variety of problems—from garbled or missing characters to an aborted initialization.

Memory testing, however, is not a simple task. Thorough memory testing typically requires sophisticated equipment such as a logic analyzer, but you can run some rough checks with your logic probe along the system's address bus.

Under normal operation, your printer's address bus is a beehive of activity. The microprocessor is constantly using the address bus to reference instructions and data. Each bit on the bus is changing continuously. On a logic probe, each address line appears as an individual clock source, as shown in Fig. 6-22. This is also true for data lines.

If a memory failure should halt your printer's operation, you might find that every address line assumes steady-state high or low values. This tells you that your processor has frozen (remember the microprocessor has control of the address bus). By reading each binary 1 or 0 on a memory device's address pins, you can determine the last address referenced. You will need manufacturer's data for your memory ICs to indicate the location and binary weight of each address bit. Try replacing RAM components in the printer. This is not a foolproof test by any means. Some printers still allow activity on the address bus even with a memory failure.

If only one (or a few) address lines appear frozen while others operate, your trouble might be elsewhere—probably in the ASIC or microprocessor.

● **Procedure 6-3** Check the microprocessor or ASIC.

This is truly the heart of the electronic control package. A microprocessor is responsible for managing the overall operation of your printer. It controls the address bus, so it directs a slave microprocessor (or ASIC), memory I/O, and communication. Naturally, a failure in the microprocessor can easily disable the entire printer.

Use your logic probe to inspect each address and data line as shown in Fig. 6-23. You should find that each line registers as an independent clock source. If you find one or more address or data lines at a steady-state logic 1 or 0, the microprocessor(s) or ASIC could be faulty. Refer to manufacturer's data to determine the address, data, and control signal locations of the microprocessor(s) or ASIC.

● **Procedure 6-4** Check the printer's communication interfaces.

Proper communication of data and commands depends not only on the printer itself, but on the printer cable, computer, and even the software in use. A problem at the computer end of your communication link can prevent the printer from working.

Parallel printers are reasonably easy to check as shown in Fig. 6-24. Use your logic probe to examine each data bit entering and leaving the data latch (or equivalent interface chip). You should see steady-state logic levels until the computer tries to send data, then you should find data bits and handshake lines acting as a clock source. If you find that data reaches the parallel interface, but does not appear on the other side, try replacing the IC. If you see that data move across the interface, your trouble might be in the microprocessor(s) (or ASIC).

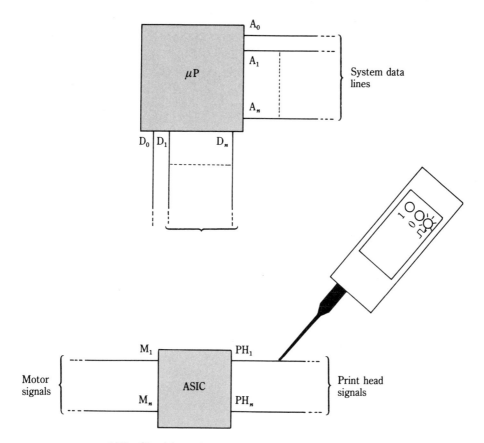

6-23   Checking microprocessor and/or ASIC signals.

Serial printers are somewhat more complex as shown in Fig. 6-25. As you saw in chapter 2, RS232 data is sent across a serial communication link in a bipolar format (the signal contains both positive and negative voltages). You can read the bipolar data by switching your logic probe to a CMOS setting to handle higher voltages, then connect a rectifier diode to the probe's tip. This orientation prevents negative voltages from damaging your logic probe, but you only see data as zeros or positive voltages.

When idle, the transmit and receive lines should assume steady-state value. If the computer sends data, the Tx and Rx lines should appear as clock sources at your line driver and receiver. A line receiver converts bipolar data to TTL levels, while a line driver converts TTL signals to bipolar levels.

Once serial data is in TTL form, it is processed by an interface IC. This may be a UART, part of an ASIC, or some other IC, but its purpose is to translate serial bits into parallel words, and vice versa. You can remove the diode from your probe, switch it back to TTL mode, and monitor data from the driver/receiver to the interface IC. Any place where the flow of data disappears is probably your trouble spot.

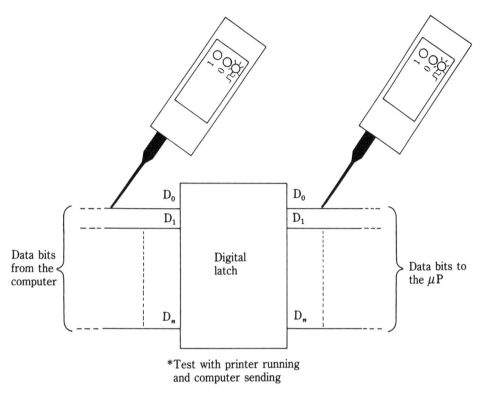

D_0
D_1
D_0
D_1

Data bits from the computer

Digital latch

Data bits to the μP

D_n
D_n

*Test with printer running
and computer sending

6-24 Checking communication—parallel.

If you cannot find a loss of data, your trouble could be in your microprocessor(s) (or ASIC).

🔵 **Procedure 6-5** Check the printer's sensors.

An ailing sensor can cause erratic operation in the printer, or prevent it from working altogether. There are three primary sensors in a conventional moving-head printer: a paper sensor, a carriage home sensor, and a carriage position encoder. Your particular printer might be equipped with others, so refer to your owner's manual for more specific information. The paper and home sensors can use either contact switches or optoisolators. You can measure the output of both types of sensors as shown in Figs. 6-26 and 6-27.

A contact switch is the most straightforward type of sensor. In one position, its output is one logic level. When actuated by contact, its output changes logic levels. You can see this by stimulating the sensor to open and close the contacts manually. If the sensor does not change output levels, it is probably defective.

An optoisolator is a bit more involved. A detector and emitter are usually mounted together in one package separated by an open slot. When paper is threaded, it interrupts the light path and the emitter exhibits one logic level. When paper is exhausted, the light path is opened. This changes the emitter's logic level

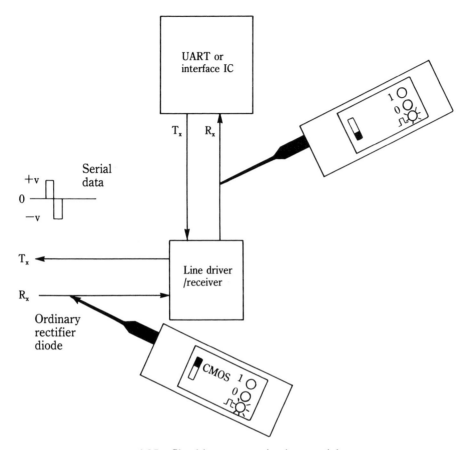

6-25 Checking communication—serial.

to indicate an error. The process works the same way for a carriage home detector. When the carriage is in its home position, it will interrupt the light path from emitter to detector, creating one logic level. Any time the carriage moves away from its home position, the light path is opened. This changes the sensor's output to another logic level. You can stimulate the sensor by inserting a small piece of paper or cardboard in the light path. If the detector's output does not change, the sensor might be defective.

You can check the output of each encoder sensor just like any ordinary optoisolator. Figure 6-28 shows this procedure in more detail. Check each sensor for a clock source by measuring each output as the carriage moves. You can initiate carriage movement through a self-test or by sending real data from the computer. Any sensor that does not produce a pulse train is probably faulty or dirty.

● **Procedure 6-6** Check the driver circuits.

Drivers convert low-power TTL signals into high-power signals needed to run devices such as motors, solenoids, or heaters. Drivers might be built onto IC chips,

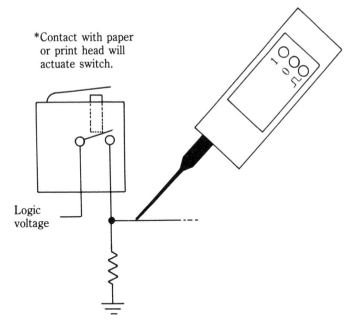

*Contact with paper
or print head will
actuate switch.

Logic
voltage

6-26   Sensor measurement—contact switch.

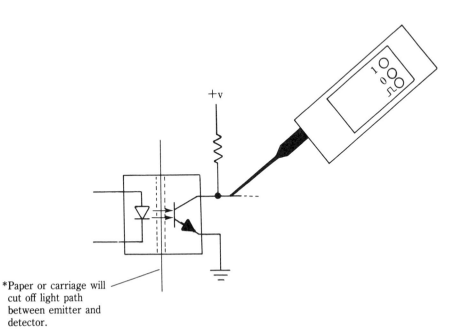

+v

*Paper or carriage will
cut off light path
between emitter and
detector.

6-27   Sensor measurement—optoisolator.

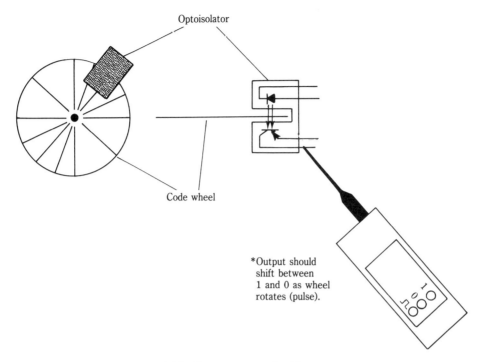

6-28 Inspector encoder bits.

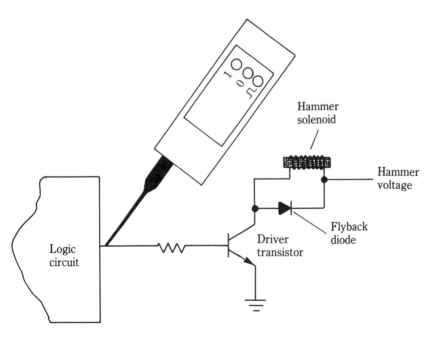

6-29 Checking driver signals.

or they could simply be discrete transistors, but the principles of testing are basically the same.

Use your logic probe to examine TTL signals entering the driver, then watch for a response at the load. Figure 6-29 shows a solenoid driver example. Main logic generates TTL pulses you can measure as a clock source with your logic probe. If you find appropriate signals entering the driver but no response at the load, either the driver (a transistor in this case) has failed, the load (a solenoid) has failed, or voltage supplying the load has failed. If you cannot detect pulses entering the driver, there might be a problem with the main logic. Be sure to inspect any questionable components before replacing the driver.

Chapter 7

Mechanics

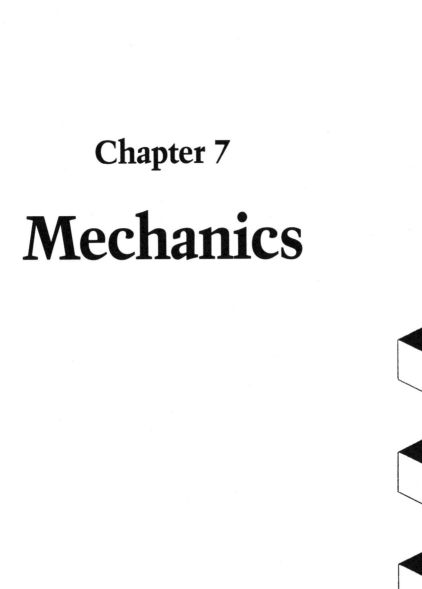

It takes more than good electronics to make a printer. A comprehensive mechanical system is needed to handle the tasks that a typical printer must perform. There are two primary mechanical systems in conventional moving-head printers: a paper transport and a print-head transport. There could also be secondary systems such as a paper cutter or ribbon transport. Line printers do not need a print-head transport because their print heads span the carriage's length. Electrostatic laser printers need a paper advance, as well as a system for mirror and drum rotation.

Understanding mechanical parts

In spite of the diversity among printer technologies, all mechanical printer systems use just about the same basic components: motors, solenoids, gears, belts, bushings, and pulleys. If you understand the principles and operation of these components, you will be able to deal with almost any printer.

Solenoids

Solenoids fall under the category of electromechanical component because they require electrical power to operate mechanical devices. All solenoids, regardless of their shape or size, operate on the principle of electromagnetism. The physics behind electromagnetism is somewhat involved, but the key principle for you to remember is whenever current passes through a wire, a magnetic field is produced around that wire. This is shown in Fig. 7-1. The intensity (or strength) of this field is directly proportional to the amount of current flowing in the conductor. Greater current results in greater magnetic strength, and vice versa.

A single strand of wire cannot generate enough magnetic force to do any useful work. Its magnetic field must be concentrated. This is accomplished by coiling the wire as shown in Fig. 7-2. When arranged in this fashion, the coil takes on magnetic poles—just like a permanent magnet. If the direction of current is reversed, magnetic polarity reverses too. To concentrate magnetic force even fur-

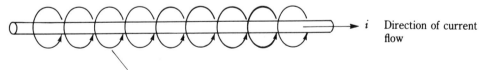

Direction of current flow

Lines of magnetic force produced by current flow

7-1 Principles of electromagnetism—magnetism in a wire.

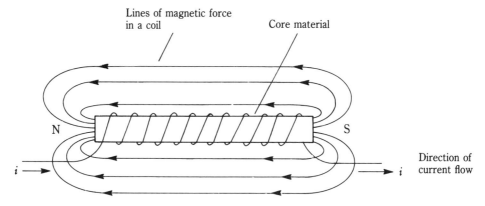

7-2 Principles of electromagnetism—magnetism in a coil.

ther, a permeable core is placed in the coil's center. Permeable materials are capable of being magnetized. Typically iron, steel, or cobalt are considered permeable, although certain ceramic-iron blends are sometimes used.

Coils can be used to form either electromagnets or solenoids. These two devices are virtually identical, but electromagnet cores remain fixed within the coil, while solenoid cores are free to move within the coil. You can use the two terms interchangeably in many circumstances, but remember there is a difference.

Electromagnets generally appear in relays to actuate one or more sets of electrical contacts as shown in Fig. 7-3. Solenoids can drive mechanical devices such as print hammers or impact print wires as in Fig. 7-4. When a solenoid coil is energized, its core (known as a *plunger*) moves. When the coil is de-energized, the spring that holds the plunger returns it to a rest position.

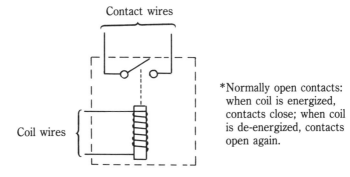

*Normally open contacts: when coil is energized, contacts close; when coil is de-energized, contacts open again.

7-3 Electromagnetic applications—relay.

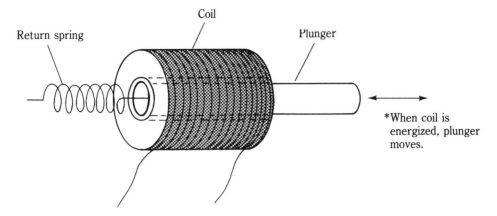

7-4 Electromagnetic applications—solenoid.

Motors

Electromagnets can be mounted around a permanent magnet assembly that is free to rotate as shown in Fig. 7-5. Altering the polarities of each motor coil (or *phase*) in the appropriate sequence, causes the permanent magnet to turn. This rotates a mechanical shaft that moves a carriage or platen.

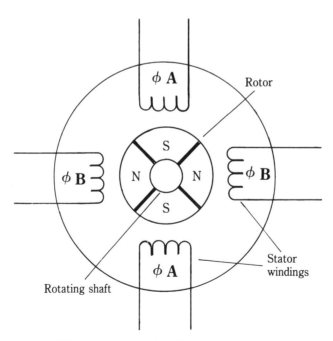

7-5 Motor principles—basic induction motor.

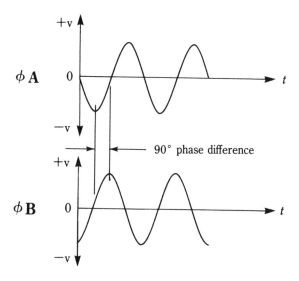

7-6 Motor principles—driver waveforms.

This type of motor, called an *induction motor*, requires two ac signals separated by 90 degrees to alternate each phase so the rotating shaft (or *rotor*) is pulled around evenly. Figure 7-6 shows a typical set of ac signals that drive an induction motor.

Induction motors are common devices, but they are rarely used in commercial printers since they are very difficult to position as precisely as today's printers

7-7 View of a stepping motor.

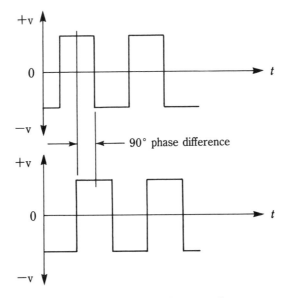

7-8   Stepping motor—driver waveforms.

demand. Instead, a variation of the induction motor, called the *stepping motor*, is used. Figure 7-7 shows a basic stepping motor.

A stepping motor is driven by a series of square waves separated by 90 degrees. This means that the rotor jumps (or steps) to a position and holds it as long as the square waves hold their conditions. Figure 7-8 shows a simple square wave sequence. In order to achieve the very small step increments that are desired, there are many more than four phases. Most commercial stepping motors are designed to provide at least 200 steps per revolution, which is less than 1.8 degrees per step. The printer's driver circuitry supplies the high-power pulses that operate stepping motors.

Other components

There are a variety of other mechanical components you should be familiar with before tackling a mechanical repair. The purpose of these additional parts is to transfer mechanical force from one place to another. For example, it could be impossible to connect a paper advance motor directly to a platen because of space limitations or some other constraint. As a result, the motor's force must be transferred from its shaft to the point where it is actually needed. Another common situation arises when force must be applied to several places at once. Instead of using multiple motors, mechanical parts can be used to split and deliver force from a single motor. Gears, pulleys, and bushings are some of the most frequently encountered parts.

Gears perform several important jobs. Their most common application is the transfer of force from one rotating shaft to another, as shown in Fig. 7-9. When two

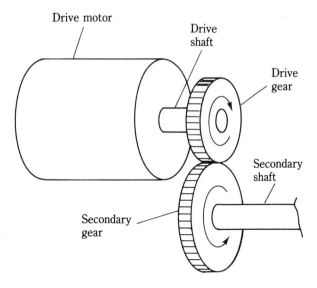

7-9   Basic gear train assembly—parallel gears.

gears are used in tandem as illustrated, the direction of the drive shaft is reversed in the secondary shaft. Additional gears can be used to distribute force among several shafts. The ratio of gear sizes can be chosen to change the speed and force of the drive motor on the secondary shaft. If the secondary gear is smaller than the drive gear, it turns faster, but with less force. If the secondary gear is larger than the drive gear, it turns slower, but with more force. Angled gears can be used to change the direction of force as shown in Fig. 7-10.

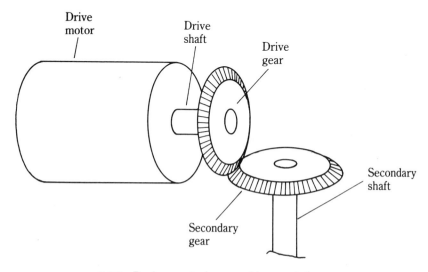

7-10   Basic gear train assembly—angled gears.

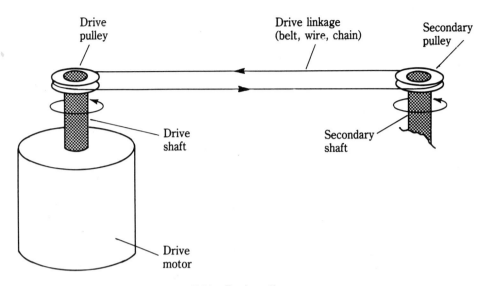

7-11 Basic pulley set.

Pulley sets are also very common. Like gears, they are used to transfer force, but pulleys use belts, cable, or chains to deliver force around the printer. Since there are no teeth to hold a cable against the pulley, there is always a chance of it sliding. For this reason, pulleys are generally used for low-force applications.

A basic pulley set is shown in Fig. 7-11. The motor turns a pulley that is little more than a wheel with a groove in it. Force is transferred to a secondary pulley through a belt or wire placed under tension—much like an ordinary belt in your automobile. As the primary pulley turns, the secondary pulley turns in the same direction. The advantage of this arrangement is that circular motion from a motor

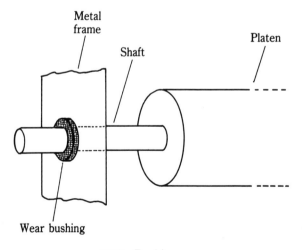

7-12 Bushings.

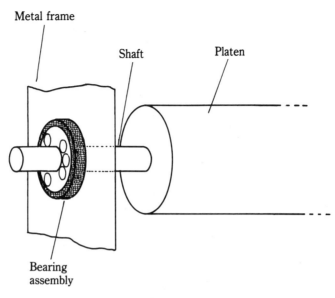

Metal frame

Shaft   Platen

Bearing
assembly

7-13   Ball bearings.

is translated into linear (left/right) motion in the belt. By connecting a point on the belt to a mechanical slide, the print head can be carried back and forth.

As with all mechanical systems, parts that are in contact with one another wear as the system runs. Lubrication with oils or grease is one solution to this problem, but lubricants harden and dry out with age. They are also notorious for collecting dust and debris from the environment. Your printer makes extensive use of bushings and bearings to reduce wear and extend the life of any load-bearing parts.

Bushings are essentially "throw away" wear surfaces that are inserted between two contacting parts, as in Fig. 7-12. A bushing is made of a material that is softer than the materials it is separating, so it will wear instead of the expensive shafts and other parts in your printer. When a bushing wears out, simply replace it. It is often easier and cheaper to replace a bushing than an entire platen or carriage rail assembly.

A bearing is an even better device for reducing mechanical wear between parts. Bearings consist of a hard metal case packed with small steel balls or rollers as shown in Fig. 7-13. Since each ball or roller contacts its load-bearing surface at one point only, friction is very low. As a result, mechanical systems do not have to work as hard to accomplish their tasks.

Paper transport

The paper transport machine mechanism is responsible for carrying paper from its supply source, past the print head, and through to the printer's output. Transport assemblies vary slightly between manufacturers, but conventional paper transports are similar to the diagram of a simple *friction feed* system shown in Fig. 7-14.

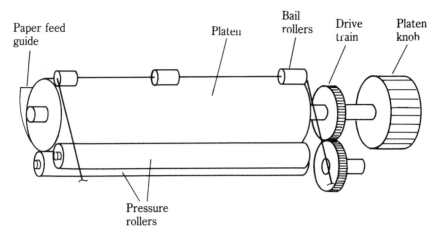

7-14   Friction feed paper transport assembly.

Paper enters the transport along a feed guide which maneuvers the sheet between a platen and one or more pressure (or pinch) rollers. Paper then moves in front of the print head assembly, and under a set of gentle bail rollers used to keep paper flat and even. There is a lever (not shown in Fig. 7-14) that releases the pressure rollers so paper can be moved freely until it is properly positioned. When the lever is engaged, paper can only be moved manually by turning the platen knob. During a paper advance, a series of square wave pulses step a drive motor. A gear assembly transfers motor force to the platen. The platen turns and paper is forced up.

Tractor feed assemblies resemble friction feed transports, but pressure rollers are replaced by a single, low-pressure contact roller and a set of sprocket wheels as shown in Fig. 7-15. A pulley arrangement is often used to connect the platen and sprocket wheels so that both turn in the same direction. Paper is inserted around the platen with little force, then engaged into the sprocket wheels.

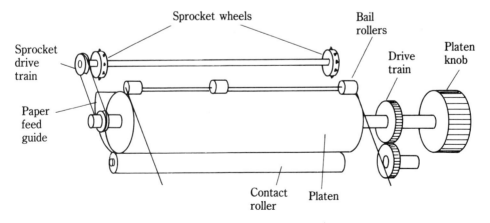

7-15   Tractor feed paper transport assembly.

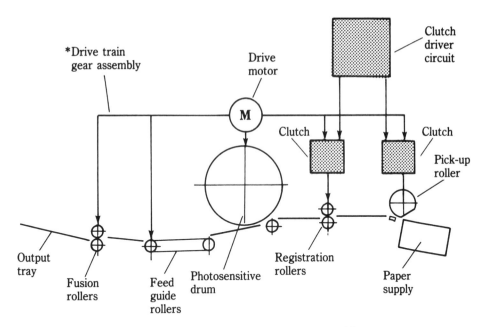

7-16   Electrostatic paper transport assembly.

Paper transport assemblies for electrostatic printers are more sophisticated, as Fig. 7-16 illustrates. A single motor usually controls the entire assembly. Its force is distributed among the various rollers through an intricate network of gears. Since the pick-up and registration rollers only run part of the time, an electro-mechanical clutch is used to engage and disengage the motor's force as needed on those rollers. Notice the photosensitive drum is included in this assembly. Of all three types of paper transport assemblies, the electrostatic assembly is the most sophisticated—and it can also offer the most problems.

Troubleshooting paper transport systems

Symptom   Paper does not feed, or feeds only intermittently. All other printer functions appear correct.

All types of paper transport mechanisms can encounter problems, especially as they grow older and undergo a significant amount of wear. When paper fails to advance properly, there are generally two sources of trouble: the paper advance motor, and its drive train.

Before you set up your multimeter, observe the paper advance drive system using Procedure 7-1 as a guide. Through time and use, drive gears and linkages can wear and shift out of alignment. This can result in intermittent movement, or a complete lack of movement. If you hear or see the paper-advance motor turning, but no platen movement is taking place, chances are good that your drive train is slipping or broken. Also check for dried or hardened lubricant that might be jamming the drive train.

If the drive train looks all right, turn your attention to the paper advance motor and its associated wiring. Procedure 7-2 explains the techniques for testing motors and solenoids. The motor might simply have failed. Its wiring might have developed an open, short, or intermittent circuit. After long periods of use, the motor shaft might have seized.

Remember the motor will not operate without a series of pulses from the printer's driver circuits. If the motor and its wiring check out, refer to chapter 6 for troubleshooting information on the electronic control package.

Symptom   The printer prints correctly, but paper walks to the left or right, or it jams or wraps around the rollers.

This type of problem is very common among friction feed and electrostatic printers. It is always related to a mechanical problem involving the rollers. Over time, wear causes rollers to shift their alignment slightly. Uneven contact pressure applies uneven friction on the page. This makes it walk one way or the other. Rollers might also be hardened from age or soiled with some foreign substance that sticks to the paper. If paper walks outside of its path, it could jam or wrap around the rollers as well. Procedure 7-3 provides steps for adjusting and rejuvenating your paper transport system.

Head transport

A head-transport mechanism (called a carriage) is used to carry the print head back and forth across a page surface. For line-print heads and electrostatic printers, there is no need to move a print head, so there is no transport.

Typically, a print head is attached to a steady mount, which is free to slide back and forth along a set of low-friction rails as shown in Fig. 7-17. A head-transport motor is mounted along the printer's frame—often adjacent to the paper-advance motor. A pulley on the motor's shaft is connected to an opposing pulley via a drive linkage that is a belt, cable, or chain. The linkage also attaches at one point to the mount. As the motor shaft rotates, linear motion is generated in the drive linkage. This, in turn, carries the mount left or right. Notice that this also turns an optical

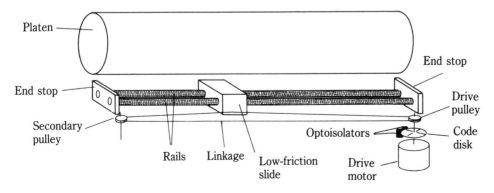

7-17   Head transport assembly.

position encoder that indicates the carriage's distance and direction to main logic. A home sensor usually mounted around the left end stop detects the carriage's home position.

Troubleshooting head transport mechanisms

Symptom The print head does not move, or moves only intermittently. All other functions appear correct.

There might be a problem with the carriage motor or motor wiring. Follow Procedure 7-2 to evaluate the condition of your head transport motor. A break in any part of the wiring harness prevents the carriage motor from turning. Even an intermittent connection can wreak havoc with the head transport. After long periods of disuse, the motor shaft might tend to stick or turn roughly. If the motor and its associated wiring appear to be intact, there could be a problem in the drive train. Procedure 7-4 guides you through an inspection of the drive train.

Remember your motor receives pulses from driver electronics. If the motor and drive system check out properly, you should check the driver signals reaching the motor. Refer to chapter 6 for a discussion of printer electronics and trouble-shooting procedures.

Symptom Print spacing is incorrect. The carriage sometimes crashes into an end stop.

When print is not spaced properly, you might be facing one of several problems. Whenever the carriage does not move as expected, your first suspicion should be a fault in the drive train. Something could be slipping or out of alignment. A loose belt or pulley can make print appear quite erratic. Procedure 7-4 guides you through a check of the carriage drive train.

A faulty carriage motor or motor wiring can also distort the horizontal print spacing. Use Procedure 7-2 to troubleshoot the motor and its wiring.

There might also be a problem with your home sensor or position encoder. The home sensor detects the slide when it reaches one side (usually the left side) of its rail assembly. When the carriage is away from its home sensor, an optical position encoder reports the carriage's direction and distance to main logic circuits. If either of these sensors should fail, the printer can lose track of where its carriage is and allow it to crash into an end stop, or position itself incorrectly. Chapter 6 covers the operation and troubleshooting of sensors.

Ribbon transport

Impact and thermal transfer printers use a ribbon to supply the ink, which is ultimately transferred to a page surface. Fabric ribbons are used exclusively with impact printers. The ribbons are long, porous strips of material that are saturated with liquid ink. They are either spooled around a ribbon bobbin (Fig. 7-18), or packed into a plastic cartridge (Fig. 7-19). Thermal transfer ribbons use a coating of dry "plastic ink" on a strip of clear plastic. Heat from a thermal print head liquifies the dry ink and transfers melted dots to the page. A typical thermal ribbon is shown in Fig. 7-20.

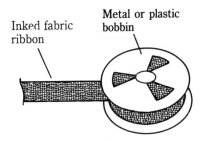

7-18 Typical spooled ribbon.

Regardless of what type of ribbon is used, it must be advanced continuously so a fresh ribbon area is always available to the print head. This is the responsibility of a ribbon transport mechanism. There are two types of ribbon transports—bidirectional and unidirectional. A bidirectional transport automatically alternates a ribbon's direction when it reaches the end of a spool. A unidirectional transport continues to advance a ribbon in one direction only. Unidirectional transports are used extensively with impact and thermal cartridge ribbons. Bidirectional transports are seldom seen any more.

Ribbon transports are generally driven from the cartridge motor, as shown in Fig. 7-21. This is a very simplified diagram. Most actual mechanisms can switch in

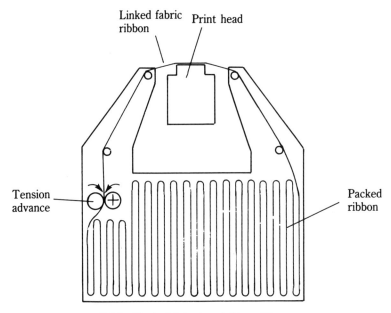

7-19 Typical inked cartridge ribbon.

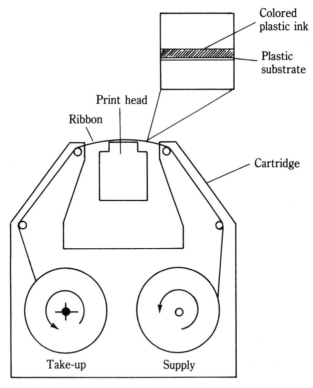

Colored
plastic ink

Plastic
substrate

Print head

Ribbon

Cartridge

Take-up

Supply

7-20 Typical thermal ribbon cartridge.

and out as the cartridge moves back and forth. In this way, ribbon is only advanced in one direction. If the mechanism is bidirectional, you also see a small switching lever (not shown in Fig. 7-21) that reverses the ribbon's direction. Ribbon transports vary greatly between printers, but you can easily recognize the mechanism by its gear shaft, which fits into the ribbon.

Troubleshooting ribbon transport mechanisms

Symptom The printer operates correctly, but print is light or nonexistent.

Do not disassemble the ribbon transport just yet. Examine the ribbon as the printer operates. See if it advances normally. If it does advance normally, inspect the ribbon itself for signs of wear and tear. It should leave ink on your fingers with just a light touch. Replace any ribbon showing signs of exhaustion. A ribbon that does not advance might be jammed within its cartridge. Pull the ribbon gently from its outlet side and see that it dispenses freely. Replace the ribbon if it is stuck.

Inspect the ribbon transport assembly as outlined in Procedure 7-5. The drive system of gears and friction wheels might be dirty or out of alignment.

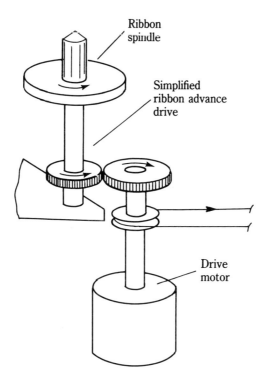

Ribbon
spindle

Simplified
ribbon advance
drive

Drive
motor

7-21 Simplified ribbon transport mechanism.

Troubleshooting procedures

Mechanical systems are usually much easier to troubleshoot than electronic circuits such as those covered in chapter 6. One major advantage is that you can easily observe the operation of a mechanical part—if a gear slips or a motor fails to turn, you can see it as it happens. Specialized test instruments are rarely needed with the exception of an occasional alignment tool or gauge.

One aspect of mechanical troubleshooting that should be stressed, however, is the extreme importance of taking *complete* notes. It is easy to confuse mechanical parts once a mechanism is disassembled. Clear, thorough notes and drawings make quick and accurate reassembly a snap. If you have parts left over, something is very wrong. Never omit parts intentionally.

○ **Procedure 7-1** Check paper transport drive train.

Remove the top cover or outer housing of your printer and observe the paper transport system during operation. Look for broken gear teeth (especially on plastic or composite gears), foreign matter in gear teeth, or gears that do not appear to mesh properly. Also check that all gears are secured to their shafts. Broken gears or other drive train parts must be replaced. Contact your printer's manufacturer for replacement parts.

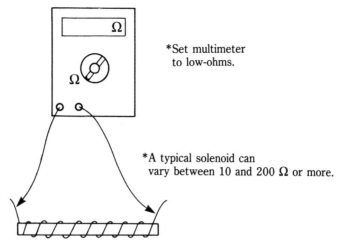

*Set multimeter
to low-ohms.

*A typical solenoid can
vary between 10 and 200 Ω or more.

7-22   Resistance check of a solenoid.

Under normal operation, the paper-advance assembly should turn freely when you turn the platen knob. Whenever you detect sticking gears or other parts, your best option is to clean them with a *nonsolvent* cleaner in order to loosen and remove foreign matter. Cleaners with harsh solvents such as acetone can easily melt plastic parts. Turn power off, then apply cleaner to the assembly with a cotton swab. Let the parts soak a bit, then remove loosened grime with another swab or a soft towel. Try to avoid disassembling the mechanism unless it is absolutely necessary. Be sure the assembly turns freely before restoring power.

Gears are usually secured to their shafts by one or more set screws. If a gear is slipping on its shaft or does not mesh correctly, it can often be adjusted by loosening its screws, aligning the gear correctly, then re-tightening the screws. Perform this procedure with all printer power off. Be sure the assembly moves freely before applying power.

● **Procedure 7-2**   Check the motor and its wiring.

Copper wire is the primary material used in motor windings and wiring. As a result, expect a motor winding to exhibit a very low (but measurable) resistance when checked with an ohmmeter. Figure 7-22 shows a basic resistance check for a coil.

Make your resistance checks with all printer power off. Set your multimeter to its lowest setting, then connect test probes across each winding as shown in Fig. 7-23. A working motor coil can be anywhere from 5 to 50 ohms depending on the wire gauge and the amount of wire used. Some motors are marked with their expected winding resistance. A very low reading could indicate a shorted winding, while a high value can suggest an open winding. In either case, the motor probably will not turn at all. Replace any defective motor.

Remember to check the integrity of all wiring that connects the motor to its driver circuits. Inspect any loose wires or connectors. Figure 7-24 shows typical

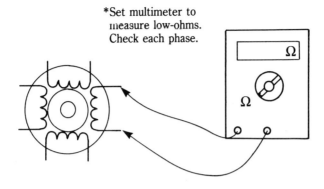

*Set multimeter to
measure low-ohms.
Check each phase.

*A typical motor winding
varies from 5 to 50 Ω.

7-23   Resistance check of a motor.

wiring checks for open and shorted wiring. Wiggle the wiring as you check to stimulate any intermittent connections. Repair or replace any defective wiring or connections.

⬤ **Procedure 7-3**   Align the rollers.

Rollers that carry paper through the paper transport mechanism can eventually fall out of alignment. This is not necessarily visible. Rollers must be perfectly
parallel and apply pressure evenly across the entire roller length. They do not have
to fall out of alignment by more than several thousandths of an inch before you
encounter problems.

In order to feed paper into the printer, pressure roller(s) must be disengaged
from the platen, then re-engaged when paper is inserted correctly. Most printers
use a mechanical lever under the tension of several springs, to actuate this movement. By adjusting the tension on each spring, contact pressure can be altered.
There are also one or more mounts that can be adjusted to keep rollers parallel.

Use extreme caution when adjusting rollers. It is *not* as easy as it looks! Every
printer is somewhat different, so proper alignment might require the use of specialized tools or measuring gauges. It might be a good idea to contact the manufacturer for alignment details before starting. Careless adjustment can do more harm
than good.

If you absolutely must attempt a mechanical adjustment without the guidance
of specific instructions or measurements tools, there are several points to keep in
mind. First, take careful note of your starting positions so you can return to a
known point if things go wrong. Second, do not adjust everything at once. Move
only one thing at a time and keep careful track of what you do. Finally, move only
in small steps. For example, if you are adjusting a screw, turn it only a fraction of a
turn, then retest the printer. This prevents you from overcompensating any single
adjustment without realizing it.

Another factor to consider is roller aging. As rubber ages, it shrinks slightly
and loses its surface friction. When this happens, paper is more likely to slip

Short circuit check

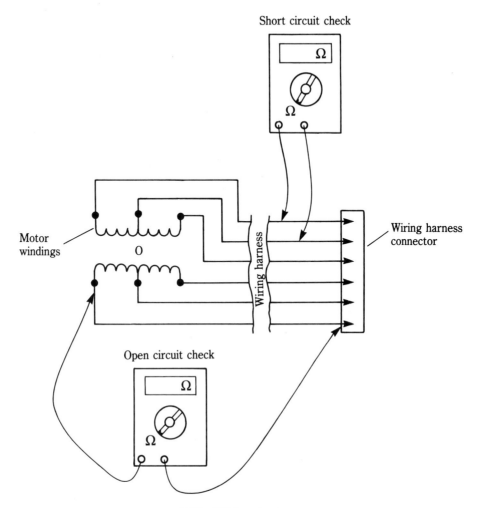

Motor
windings

Wiring harness
connector

Wiring harness

Open circuit check

7-24 Wiring checks.

between rollers instead of being pulled through. Rubber can be revitalized with special solvents made just for platens. These solvents are available through just about any comprehensive stationary store. Two name brands and manufacturers of platen solvents are listed in appendix D.

○ **Procedure 7-4** Check the head transport drive train.

There are two areas of the head transport that you should pay close attention to: the drive linkages, and the low-friction slide. Refer to Fig. 7-17 for an illustration of a typical print head transport system.

Most drive linkages (wires, belts, or chains) eventually stretch under tension. As they stretch, they loosen around their pulleys. This can cause random or erratic slipping—the linkage can even fall off. Even though the drive motor turns just fine, you see poor character spacing and head positioning. Check the alignment and tension of your drive train. Be sure all parts are tight, but still turn freely. Adjust

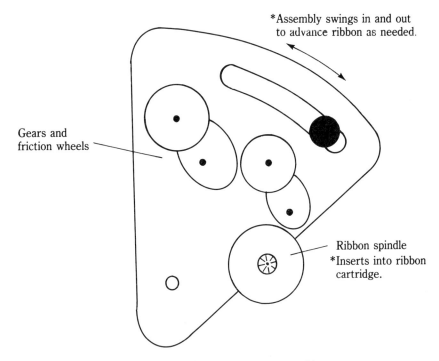

*Assembly swings in and out
to advance ribbon as needed.

Gears and
friction wheels

Ribbon spindle
*Inserts into ribbon
cartridge.

7-25   Typical ribbon transport assembly.

sion on the take-up pulley if necessary. Replace any belt, wire, or chain that appears damaged or worn out.

The low-friction slide can also present problems due to age, lack of routine maintenance, or physical abuse. If any slide rail(s) become misaligned, the slide itself can bind or jam. You might or might not be able to adjust the alignment of your slides—it depends upon your particular printer. Bearings or bushings in the slide could simply be worn. Check this by observing how much play there is in the mount. It should be fixed tightly to its rails, but move freely left or right. Realign or replace the slide rail assembly as necessary. You might need specialized tools or measuring gauges to align the slide properly.

● **Procedure 7-5**   Check the ribbon transport system.

Remove the ribbon from your printer. You will see a small sprocket gear that inserts into the ribbon cartridge (or spool). Grouped just below the sprocket, you will see the other gears and friction wheels that make up the ribbon transport mechanism. This can be mounted near the left side of the head transport assembly, or close to the print head. A typical ribbon transport assembly is shown in Fig. 7-25.

Run the printer without its ribbon and observe the ribbon transport. Use caution when running a ribbon. Some print heads (especially thermal transfer) can be damaged from friction against a paper surface. Check your owner's manual for specific cautions before running without a ribbon. You might also have to perform some partial printer disassembly to see the entire ribbon transport.

Look for any gears or friction rollers that might be sticking or jammed together. Dust and oils from paper and ink can build up in the mechanism. Clean away accumulations of dust and dirt with a nonsolvent cleaner. Wipe off grime with a clean, soft cloth. Also check for parts that appear to be slipping or loose. Each ribbon transport is a little bit different, so you might or might not be able to tighten and adjust the parts in your particular mechanism. A worn out ribbon transport might have to be replaced entirely.

Chapter 8

Routine maintenance

There are two types of maintenance that you can perform on your printer. Most of this book has been devoted to the area of repair maintenance—dealing with a problem *after* it has surfaced. Preventive maintenance, however, is intended to stop potential problems *before* they occur.

Why routine maintenance is a good idea

Regardless of what type of printer you own (impact, thermal, ink jet, or electrostatic) it contains three general types of components: electronic, mechanical, and disposable.

Disposable parts—just as the name implies—are parts or materials that can be discarded when their usefulness is exhausted. Paper, ribbons, toner cartridges, and ink cartridges are four of the most familiar disposables.

Electronic components and assemblies are used in the printer's power supply and electronic control package. As a general rule, electronic parts either work or they do not. There is no in-between, so there is no real routine maintenance that can be performed short of keeping the printer clean, dry, away from excessive heat, cold, or vibration—any physical factors that could damage delicate circuit board electronics.

Mechanical parts comprise the portions of the printer that do the physical work. Physical work results in wear and tear, so this is where preventive maintenance steps are concentrated. Print heads, paper transports, and print head transports are just some of the mechanical systems that require periodic preventive maintenance procedures.

Unlike electrical devices, mechanical parts can sustain a lot of abuse before they finally break down. Unfortunately, the adverse effects of wear and the operating environment degrade print quality long before a complete failure. By regularly following a series of routine mechanical adjustments, cleaning, and (limited) lubrication, you can maintain the quality of print and extend the working life of your printer.

Adjustments

Adjustments involve changing such things as spacing, tension, or alignment. Keep several important factors in mind before attempting to make adjustments. First, only perform adjustments on an "as needed" basis. If a printer is performing adequately, there is no need to adjust anything. (There is an old axiom in troubleshooting that says, "if it isn't broken, don't fix it.") Second, be sure you have the appropriate tools (and measurement gauges when needed) to perform the adjustment. Your owner's manual probably tells you if there are any special tools needed. Finally, if you absolutely must attempt an adjustment "by eye," take careful note of your starting point so you will have a known place to return to just in case the adjustment fails or degrades the printer's operation.

Adjusting print head spacing

Impact print heads must be held at a certain distance from the platen in order for them to operate properly. As the print head moves farther from a platen, its print will appear lighter. Most printers have a built-in head spacing lever to allow for differences in paper thickness or ribbon freshness. A print head should also be perfectly parallel to the platen at all times.

If your printer does not have a head adjustment lever, or is no longer parallel to the platen, you can adjust the head as shown in Fig. 8-1 or Fig. 8-2. Most impact print heads should be adjusted to a position between 0.3 and 0.7 millimeters from a platen (about 0.5 mm average). Use a "feeler gauge" to measure this distance. You may obtain a feeler gauge from a local hardware or automotive supply store. The head can be moved in or out by adjusting one or more of its carriage rails as in Fig. 8-1, or by adjusting the head on its carriage slide as in Fig. 8-2.

Check your new distance with the carriage positioned at the left, middle, and right. Be sure to measure the same distance all the way across. Run the printer in its self-test mode to ensure that the print appears clear and consistent across every line. If print still appears light, re-check your head alignment. If print is now too dark, or print wires penetrate the page, pull back the print head with its distance adjustment lever, or readjust the head.

Note that some ink jet printers can be adjusted in a very similar manner. Thermal print heads are always in contact with the page surface, so only their contact tension needs to be adjusted. Electrostatic printers do not offer any sort of print head spacing adjustment for their image formation systems.

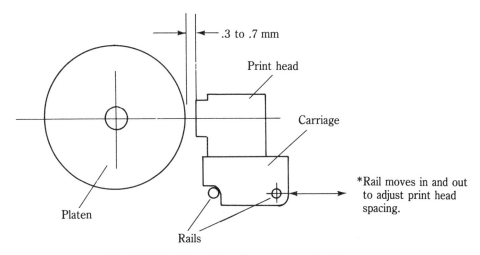

8-1 Print head spacing adjustment—rail adjustment.

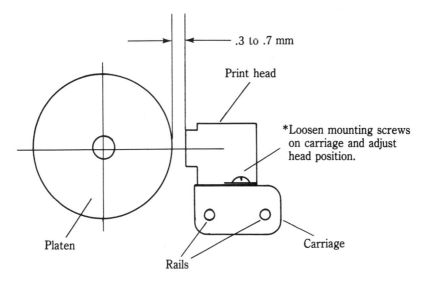

8-2   Print head spacing adjustment—carriage adjustment.

Adjusting linkage tension

The print head transport system's drive linkage (either a belt, wire, or chain) is constantly under tension. After a great deal of age and use, the linkage tends to elongate. As it does, it loosens around its pulleys, and this can result in a slipping carriage or poor dot spacing. Many pulley-driven systems offer a simple means of adjusting linkage tension, as shown in Fig. 8-3.

The drive side of the pulley arrangement consists of a drive motor, drive pulley, take-up pulley, and linkage. Take-up pulleys are normally held fixed, but the drive

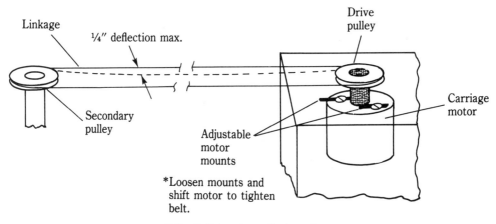

8-3   Belt tension adjustment.

motor is usually mounted to a metal frame with slots that allow the position of the motor (and drive pulley) to be shifted slightly. In this way, tension can be maintained in the linkage. Move the carriage home and gently press on the linkage. This causes a deflection as shown in Fig. 8-3. Less than 0.25 inches of deflection is generally acceptable. Be careful when adjusting tension. It can easily be accomplished by eye, but do not apply *too* much tension. This simply wears out your drive pulleys.

Cleaning and lubrication

While adjustments should be made only when needed, the printer should be cleaned and lubricated regularly to keep its mechanical parts running smoothly. There are five steps you should perform in this routine for most moving-head printers: clean the printer, clean the rollers, clean and lubricate the print head, clean and lubricate the paper transport, and clean and lubricate the head transport. With a little practice, these steps can be performed correctly in under an hour.

Clean the printer

Your printer is going to accumulate dust and dirt on its outer case, as well as inside its carriage area. Just how much dust accumulates depends on its operating environment. A clean, professional office might not carry much dust to the printer at all, while a rough industrial environment (like a manufacturing plant floor) can subject the printer to tremendous amounts of dust, dirt, grime, and any other airborne gunk that could be present. Over time, this accumulation works its way into every mechanism and causes slipping gears or belts, or even blocking of optical sensors. A little time spent cleaning the printer now can save a lot more time (and frustration) later when something goes wrong.

Start by turning the printer off. Clean the outer case with a soft cloth *lightly* dampened with clean water. *Never* spray water or cleaner directly onto the case or outer covers. Stubborn stains can be removed using a little very mild household detergent sprayed on or touched to a cloth. *Never* use solvent-based cleaners to attack a stain. They attack the cover plastic instead. Use extra care to keep moisture away from the control panel.

Remove carriage covers from the top of your printer as in Fig. 8-4, and vacuum away any dirt or dust inside. If gunk still adheres inside the printer, loosen it with a medium-bristled brush and vacuum it away. Some manufacturers sell small, handheld vacuums for this task, but any household vacuum with a flexible nozzle should do. Be careful not to change any dip switch settings with the nozzle or brush while you are vacuuming.

Clean the rollers

Anything that can find its way into a carriage area can also work into your rollers, so it is always a good idea to clean and rejuvenate the rollers as part of a routine maintenance regimen.

8-4 View of carriage cavity.

Turn off all printer power, then remove any paper in the paper transport. Simple dust and ordinary stains can usually be removed with a soft, water-dampened cloth, and a little effort. Clean the platen by rubbing back and forth across its length while turning the platen knob by hand. This is illustrated in Fig. 8-5. Continue cleaning the platen through several revolutions. This helps to pick up and

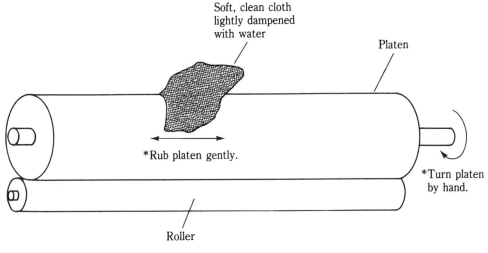

8-5 Cleaning the rollers.

carry away any gunk that might have worked its way into pressure rollers. Avoid any sort of detergent or solvent (except for specific platen solvents) on your rollers.

For a superior cleaning, use a cleaning agent formulated specifically for use on platens. Many quality stationary stores carry this type of chemical. It was originally intended for typewriter rollers, but it has the same effect on printer rollers. It not only does an excellent cleaning job, but also rejuvenates the texture and integrity of the rubber. In friction feed paper transports, roller quality plays an important role. Use only high-quality solvents and follow the manufacturer's directions exactly.

Clean and lubricate the print head

Although thermal print heads do not require routine cleaning, impact and ink jet heads should be cleaned regularly. You learned about the basic construction and operation of these heads in chapter 4.

Paper is made up of small, tightly interwoven fibers bonded together at a mill by chemicals, temperature, and pressure. Every time an impact print head strikes a page through an inked ribbon, the impact liberates some of those fibers. Most of these microscopic fibers settle into the carriage area just like any other dust particle present in the open air, but some fibers combine with ribbon ink to form a kind of sticky glue. This glue can eventually work its way into print wires and cause them to jam.

If you wipe away this accumulation from the print head's face every time you change the ribbon, jams due to gunk buildup are virtually eliminated. You can

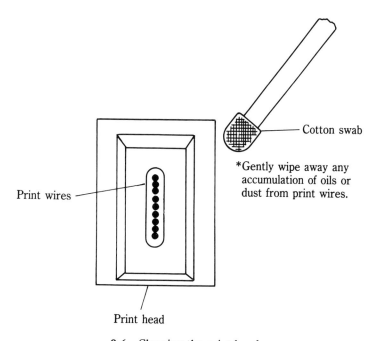

Print wires

Cotton swab

*Gently wipe away any accumulation of oils or dust from print wires.

Print head

8-6 Cleaning the print head.

probably just unclip your print head from its carriage holder for a clear view of the face. Wipe the print wires with a dry cotton swab, or one dipped in alcohol or very light household oil, as shown in Fig. 8-6. If you do this before any accumulation can dry out and harden, it should wipe off with little or no effort. Never use harsh solvents to clean a print head. They can damage plastic components.

Print wires that are already jammed or heavily contaminated can be cleared easily, as shown in Fig. 8-7. Gently extend each print wire one at a time and clean around each wire with a fresh cotton swab dipped in very light household oil. Be *very* careful here since wires are relatively delicate, and only extend a few millimeters. Do not yank on a print wire or use excessive force, which can bend a wire. Work each wire and continue cleaning until all of them move freely.

Since ink jets apply ink by "squirting" droplets onto a page, no part of the head ever actually touches a page. Much less dust is generated this way; however, ink jets must provide a clear path for ink to flow. Any obstructions can easily clog a nozzle. This presents you with a slightly different set of cleaning problems.

Liquid ink is typically an indelible, solvent-based chemical that does not readily evaporate in open air. Any residual ink within the nozzles can remain exposed to air for prolonged periods of time (maybe a week or so) without risk of drying out and clogging. The home position of many ink jet printers also has a loose cover that helps to cover each nozzle during periods of disuse. No matter how well the ink is formulated, or how tightly nozzles are covered, *long* periods of disuse can allow ink to dry and clog (even partially) in one or more nozzles. A clog must either be wiped away or purged from inside.

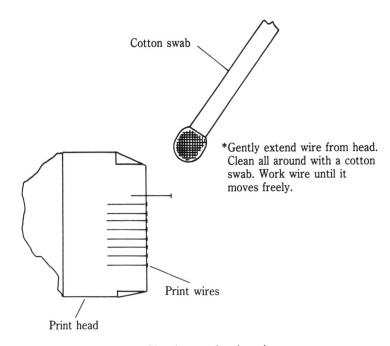

8-7   Cleaning stuck print wires.

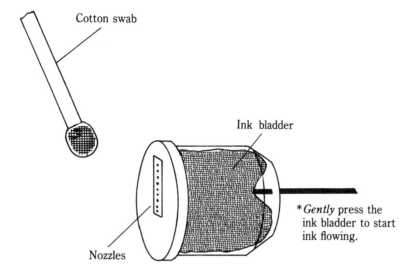

Cotton swab

Ink bladder

*Gently press the ink bladder to start ink flowing.

Nozzles

8-8 Cleaning a replaceable ink jet head.

A replaceable ink jet head can be unclipped from its carriage mount for a clear view of the face. Clean away any accumulation of dried ink from each nozzle with a dry soft cloth or cotton swab, then use the wooden end to press gently on the ink bladder. You should see ink bead up on each nozzle, as shown in Fig. 8-8. The force should be enough to overcome hardened ink, but be careful not to puncture the ink bladder. Repeat this several times until all ink nozzles are clear. If this fails to clear the condition, replace the ink head cartridge.

Some ink jet heads must be purged with a cleaning solvent that dissolves dried ink. This option is generally available in nonreplaceable heads, as illustrated in Fig. 8-9. Printers with this type of head come with some sort of cleaning or purging kit. It might consist of a syringe and a container of cleaner, or it could offer something more elaborate. Fill the syringe with cleaner, attach it to the head's ink or purge inlet, then gently force cleaner into the ink reservoir. As cleaner flows in, it acts to reduce ink viscosity and it will flow easily from the nozzles. *This makes a terrific mess!* Have a pair of rubber gloves and plenty of paper towels around before attempting a purge. Continue to inject cleaner (it might take more than one syringe full) into the head until all ink has been evacuated and only cleaner is flowing. You might need to let the cleaner sit and dissolve the clog for a while before it clears. Check your manufacturer's cleaning instructions for specific details and procedures.

Clean and lubricate the paper transport

The paper transport drive train can eventually become dusty and dirty enough to cause jamming or slipping gears. To combat this, the paper transport drive should be cleaned and lubricated regularly.

Turn off all printer power and expose the paper drive train. You will probably have to remove the printer's top cover to get an unobstructed view, as shown in

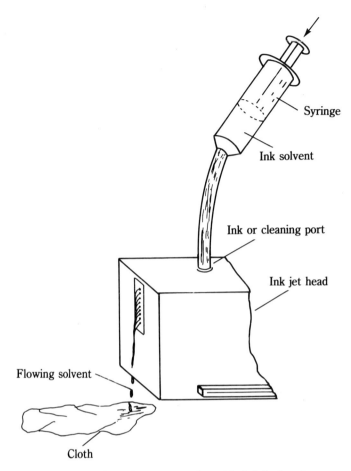

Syringe

Ink solvent

Ink or cleaning port

Ink jet head

Flowing solvent

Cloth

8-9 Cleaning a non-replaceable ink jet head.

Fig. 8-10. There might be an additional guard or shield in place to cover the gear train. If there is, it must be removed as well. Clean each gear carefully with a soft cloth dampened with a very mild, nonsolvent cleaner. Use a cotton swab if necessary to clean between gear teeth. If you *must* disassemble the gear train to clean properly, be certain to make careful note of how everything goes together. Never use harsh cleaners or solvents to remove dirt and debris from components.

Lubrication should be reapplied to the gear train *only* if it was lubricated to begin with. Ideally, you should use the same type of lubricant, but a light household oil usually works in a pinch. Place a few drops into the teeth of one or more gears, then turn the platen knob to rotate the gear assembly. This spreads a thin layer of oil evenly through the drive train. Continue to add oil until every gear shows a light, consistent coating. Never douse the gear train in oils, or use heavy oils or grease (unless specifically requested in your user's manual). This just attracts more gunk that will be harder to clean the next time around.

8-10 View of a gear train assembly.

Clean and lubricate the head transport

A carriage mount rides along two or more low-friction rails. These rails are typi-cally made of hardened steel (stainless steel is very expensive) and ground to a smooth finish. Through a combination of humidity, dust, and dirt, rails corrode and add friction to the slide. This tends to slow the carriage down. In extreme cases, it can bind the carriage and interfere with character spacing. It is important to keep these rails clean at all times.

Wipe each rail with a clean, soft cloth to remove any dust or debris. Rust can be swept away with a light touch of steel wool, but remember that rust and steel wool fibers can short out electronic components. Be sure to vacuum away all loose rust or fibers before reapplying power.

Place a few drops of light household oil onto each rail, then move the carriage back and forth to distribute the oil evenly. A light coating of oil helps to protect the metal rails from further corrosion. Never use heavy oils or grease on your rails; they simply attract more dust and dirt.

Electrostatic printer maintenance

As you might imagine, not all of the cleaning procedures discussed so far work with electrostatic printers. Electrostatic printers require their own special cleaning

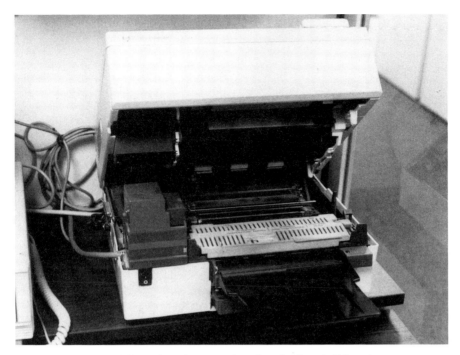

8-11   View of an electrostatic printer's clamshell housing.

and lubrication steps. Three common steps are: clean the printer and rollers, clean the optics, and clean the corona wires.

Clean the printer and rollers

You can clean the electrostatic printer just as you would clean any other printer. Use a clean, soft cloth lightly dampened with water. Stubborn stains can often be removed by adding a mild household detergent to the cloth. Never put water or cleaners directly on the printer's case.

Open your printer as you would to change the EP cartridge. Some printers use a "clamshell" design that opens in two halves, as shown in Fig. 8-11. This exposes your photosensitive drum, corona wires, some rollers, and many of your drive gears. Depending on how your particular printer is designed, it may also expose the laser and shutter (if it is a laser-type writing mechanism). Dust and debris are much less likely to accumulate inside an electrostatic printer because of the way it is enclosed, but you should brush or vacuum away any accumulations of toner particles in exposed areas. It might help you to remove the EP cartridge to protect the drum and primary corona from accidental damage.

Rollers can be cleaned as much as you would clean rollers on conventional printers. Rub away dust or debris with a soft cloth dampened lightly with water. Do not soak the rollers! Use caution when cleaning the rollers. Be sure that all printer power is off and allow enough time for fusion rollers to cool down. Remember electrostatic printers are very delicate devices. Do not bump anything out of alignment.

Clean the optics

Any dust or debris that accumulates on an optical lens can have a serious impact on the quality of electrostatic print. Anything that interferes with the light path of a writing mechanism can easily obscure part or all of the writing process. Simple dust can be blown off lenses and shutters with a can of photography-grade compressed air available from any professional photography store.

For fingerprints, stains, or anything else that compressed air will not blow away, optical components can be cleaned with photography-grade, lint-free wipes and cleaning fluid specially formulated to clean optical lenses. *Never* use water, cleaners, or any other kind of fluid to clean your optical components. These can streak and leave a residue that does more damage than the dirt you are trying to remove. Refer to your owner's manual for information on optics and their placement.

Clean the corona wires

In order for a corona wire to maintain an even charge field across its entire length, it must be perfectly clean all the way across. The problem is that high-voltage

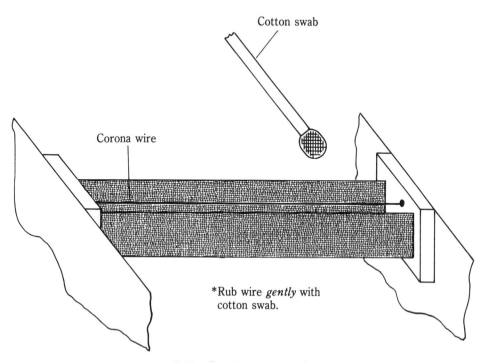

8-12   Cleaning corona wires.

attracts dust and dirt that adhere to the wire and form patches of gunk that create a sort of insulation. These "insulated" patches of wire cannot produce the same amount of charge that clean wire can. As a result, certain areas of the drum or page might not receive the image or transfer toner properly. These appear as light or washed-out streaks traveling the length of the page.

Clean the primary and transfer corona wire as shown in Fig. 8-12. Turn off all printer power and gently rub away any residue with a clean cotton swab dipped lightly in water or alcohol. You can also use a special-purpose cleaning tool supplied with some types of electrostatic printers. As you clean, avoid monofilament strings wrapped around the transfer corona. If you break this protective strapping, it will have to be replaced before the printer is used again. Use extra care when cleaning the primary corona. Since it is a part of the EP cartridge, it is thinner and much more fragile than the transfer corona. If you break it, the entire EP cartridge must be replaced.

Service intervals

For preventive maintenance to have any positive effect on the longevity of your printer, you must perform it properly and regularly. Unfortunately, there is little agreement on just when to perform each check or cleaning. Different printer manufacturers offer their own recommendations. Remember a printer's reliability depends on two major factors: how much the printer is used, and what environment the printer is used in. For example, a lightly used printer in a clean environment does not need the same maintenance as a heavily used printer in a hostile environment.

Under most circumstances, a typical printer should receive preventive maintenance whenever a ribbon or an EP cartridge is changed. This holds true for most office, home, or store environments that are reasonably clean, warm, and dry. If you discover an accumulation of debris before it is necessary to change the ribbon, perform maintenance even more often.

Harsh environments (such as factories), where temperatures can be extreme, and airborne contaminants can build up rapidly, demand more frequent attention. How frequent this attention should be depends on just how harsh the environment is. Check for buildups once a month and perform maintenance if necessary. If buildup is substantial, perform maintenance even more frequently.

Appendix A
Troubleshooting charts

Print head mechanisms: Character impact print heads

Symptoms		Procedures
Printing quality has become poor. Printed characters appear broken, tilted, missing, or otherwise distorted.	○	Procedure 4-1
Printed characters appear faded at the top or bottom.	○	Procedure 4-2
The print head assembly moves back and forth across the page, but print is light or nonexistent. The hammer does not appear to fire.	◖	Procedure 4-3
The print head assembly moves back and forth across the page, but it does not print. The hammer does not fire, but a die rotates normally.	◖	Procedure 4-3
The print head assembly moves back and forth across the page, but print is intermittent. Characters might be jumbled.	◖	Procedure 4-4

Print head mechanisms: Dot-matrix impact print heads

Symptoms	Procedures
The print head assembly moves back and forth across the page, but it does not print. None of the print wires appear to fire.	◒ Procedure 4-5
The print head moves back and forth across the page, but printing is intermittent. Wires appear to fire erratically.	● Procedure 4-4
The print head fires, but there are one or more white (missing) or black lines through the print.	◒ Procedure 4-6 ● Procedure 4-7
Printing is correct, but it appears faint.	Check ribbon, ribbon advance, and head position.

Print head mechanisms: Thermal print heads

Symptoms	Procedures
The paper and carriage (if used) advance normally, but the print is intermittent or nonexistent.	◒ Procedure 4-4 ◒ Procedure 4-5
The paper and carriage (if used) advance normally, but there are white (missing) or black lines running through the print.	◒ Procedure 4-5 ● Procedure 4-7

Print head mechanisms: Ink jet print heads

Symptoms	Procedures
The print head assembly moves back and forth, but it does not print, or it prints only intermittently.	◒ Procedure 4-4 ● Procedure 4-5
The print head assembly moves back and forth, but there are one or more white (missing) or black lines running through the print.	◒ Procedure 4-4 ● Procedure 4-7
The print being produced is faint or smudged.	Check for clogged nozzles Check paper type.

Print head mechanisms: Electrostatic printing

Symptoms	Procedures
Printed images are faint, light, or appear washed out.	○ Procedure 4-8 ● Procedure 4-9

Printed images are excessively
dark or all black.

○ Procedure 4-8
◖ Procedure 4-9

Printing intensity is correct, but
random smudges are occurring.

Check the drum.
Check the rollers.

Printing appears to be correct, but
there are white (light) or black
stripes along the length of the page, or
"speckles" that appear consistently on every
page.

Check the drum.
Check fusing rollers.

Images appear to be distorted. They
might appear too short, too tall, wavy, or
light and out of focus.

Check the drum and drum motor.
Check the mirror and mirror
motor.

Power supplies

Symptoms		**Procedures**
The power supply is completely dead. No power indicators are lit and the printer does not function at all.	◓ ●	Procedure 5-1 Procedure 5-2
Power supply operation is intermittent.	◖	Procedure 5-3
The power indicator is lit, but the printer is not working or not (working properly).	◖ ● ◖	Procedure 5-1 Procedure 5-2 Procedure 5-3

Electronics: Main logic

Symptoms		**Procedure**
The printer's power indicator is lit, but it fails to initialize. There is no apparent activity in the printer after power is turned on. The self-test mode does not work.	◖ ● ●	Procedure 6-1 Procedure 6-2 Procedure 6-3
The printer appears to initialize, but it does not print under computer control. Self-test checks correctly.	●	Procedure 6-4
The printer initializes, but it does not print. The "paper out" indicator is lit even though paper is threaded.	◖	Procedure 6-5
The printer prints, but its print is garbled or erratic. The self-test checks properly.	●	Procedure 6-4

Electronics: I/O drivers

Symptoms		Procedures
The printer prints as expected, but one or more white (missing) or black lines are running through the print.	●	Procedure 6-6
The carriage or paper advance does not appear to operate. This symptom persists during a self-test.	●	Procedure 6-6
The printer prints, but its carriage positions erratically or incorrectly. This persists during a self-test.	◒	Procedure 6-5

Mechanics: Paper transport

Symptoms		Procedures
Paper does not feed, or feeds only intermittently. All other printer functions appear to be correct.	○ ◐	Procedure 7-1 Procedure 7-2
The printer prints correctly, but paper walks to the left or right, or it jams or wraps around the rollers.	◒	Procedure 7-3

Mechanics: Head transport

Symptoms		Procedures
The print head does not move, or moves only intermittently. All other functions appear to be correct.	◐ ○	Procedure 7-2 Procedure 7-4
Print spacing is incorrect. The carriage might sometimes crash into an end stop.	◐ ○	Procedure 7-2 Procedure 7-4

Mechanics: Ribbon Transport

Symptoms		Procedures
The printer operates correctly, but print is light or nonexistent.	●	Procedure 7-5

Appendix B
Soldering techniques

Soldering is the most commonly used method of connecting wires and components within an electrical or electronic circuit. Two or more wires (or component leads) are heated and joined together with a molten metal. This forms a tight, lasting inter-molecular bond that is mechanically strong, as well as electrically sound. All that is needed is a low-wattage, electronics-grade soldering pencil and solder.

Technically speaking, solder is an alloy that contains several metals. Various types of solder are available, but you should *only* use electronic solder for printer repair. Electronic solder is an alloy of 60 percent tin and 40 percent lead (known as "60/40" solder) that is pliable and melts at relatively low temperatures. It also contains a chemical core of rosin that cleans the metal surfaces to be joined. This allows solder to adhere better and form an even tighter bond.

Before you solder, clean the tip of your hot iron by rubbing it into a sponge soaked with clean water, then apply a light coating of fresh solder to the tip. This is called "tinning" the iron. A fresh layer of solder helps to transfer the iron's heat to the joint. Tin the iron whenever its tip becomes dirty or blackened. You may have to do this every few joints.

When soldering, heat both surfaces to be joined. If you are solderng two wires, use the tip to heat both wires together. If you are soldering a component into a printed circuit board, heat the component's lead and printer circuit pad together. As the joint heats, flow solder into the joint while the iron is still applied. Make sure that solder flows cleanly and evenly into the joint. Remove the solder and iron and allow the joint to cool. Do not move the joint until solder has set after a few seconds. A good solder joint exhibits a smooth, even, silver appearance.

Solder does not flow unless the joint is hot. If it is not, solder cools before it bonds. This forms a "cold" solder joint which results in a rough, dull, gray appearance, and does not make a good electrical or mechanical bond. A cold solder joint can be corrected simply by reheating the faulty joint and adding fresh solder.

You might find it helpful to tin both parts of the joint separately *before* actually soldering them together. This is especially helpful when making large, heavy-duty wire connections. Prepare each wire or component lead, heat it with your iron, then apply solder to the wire. If you are tinning a solid wire or component lead, just apply a light coating or solder to the lead's surface. If you are tinning a stranded wire, apply enough solder to bond each strand together. After all parts of the joint have been tinned, solder them together normally. You will find that solder flows better when each part has been tinned in advance.

There are several things to keep in mind when soldering. First, *always wear a pair of safety glasses to protect your eyes!* Beads of molten solder can be launched by a slipping wire or component lead, and can do serious damage to your eyes. Next, use a low-wattage soldering pencil instead of a high-wattage gun. You need only 25 to 30 watts to do electronic soldering. Third, *never* use plumber's solder (also called *acid-core* solder) for electronics work. Acid cleans the joint just as well as rosin, but after the joint is soldered, trapped acid continues to dissolve metal and ruins the connection from within. The joint will fail, and it is almost impossible to detect. Use only $60/40$ electronics-grade solder. Finally, be careful how much heat you apply to a joint. It should take only a few seconds to heat, solder, and cool a joint. If you leave the soldering iron on the joint for a long time, wire insulation begins to melt away. Excessive heat can easily destroy semiconductor components such as transistors or integrated circuits.

Appendix C
Electronic components

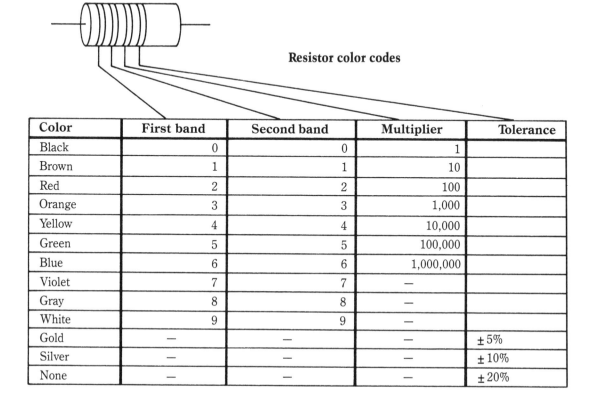

Resistor color codes

Color	First band	Second band	Multiplier	Tolerance
Black	0	0	1	
Brown	1	1	10	
Red	2	2	100	
Orange	3	3	1,000	
Yellow	4	4	10,000	
Green	5	5	100,000	
Blue	6	6	1,000,000	
Violet	7	7	—	
Gray	8	8	—	
White	9	9	—	
Gold	—	—	—	± 5%
Silver	—	—	—	± 10%
None	—	—	—	± 20%

Ceramic capacitor markings

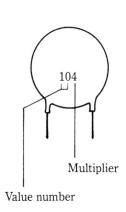

Value number

Multiplier

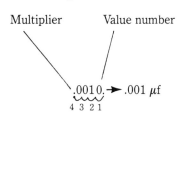

Multiplier

Value number

Resistor

Potentiometer

Rheostat

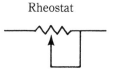

Fixed capacitor

Adjustable capacitor

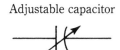

Coil: air core

Coil: solid core

Transformer

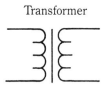

dc voltage source

ac voltage source

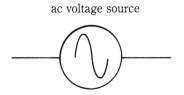

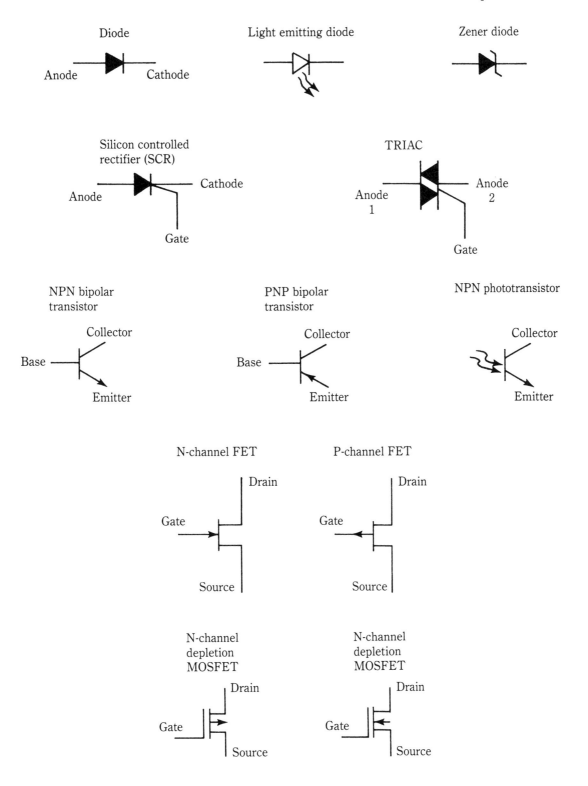

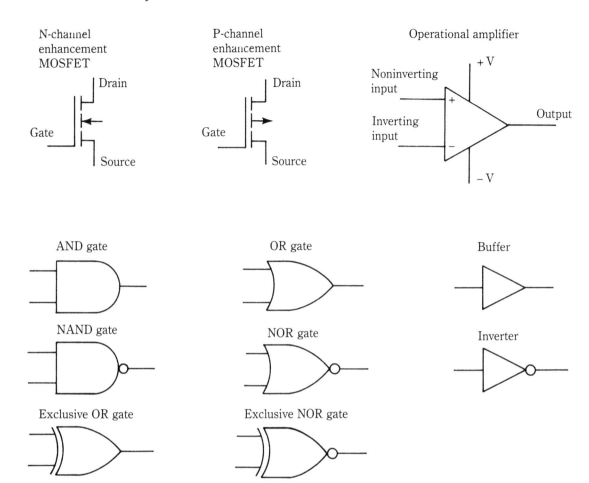

Appendix D
Parts and Supplies Vendors

Active Electronics, Inc.
11 Cummings Park
Woburn, MA 01801
(800) 677-8899
(617) 932-4616

Active stocks many domestic electronic components, along with books, tools, and supplies.

Consolidated Electronics, Inc.
705 Watervliet Ave.
Dayton, OH 45420
(800) 543-3568
(513) 252-5662

Consolidated stocks a wide assortment of electronic parts, tools, and supplies.

Dalbani Corporation of America
2733 Carrier Ave.
Los Angeles, CA 90040
(800) 325-2264
(213) 727-0054

Dalbani offers a variety of domestic and foreign electronic components, as well as mechanical parts.

Eiger Electronics
91 Toledo St.
Farmingdale, NY 11735
(800) 835-8316

Eiger stocks electronic components and subassemblies for commercial electronic products.

ESP (Electronic Service Parts)
2901 E. Washington St.
Indianapolis, IN 46201
(800) 382-9976
(317) 269-1527

ESP stocks electronic components and subassemblies for commercial electronic products, as well as a selection of tools and supplies.

Howard W. Sams & Company
2647 Waterfront Parkway East Drive
Indianapolis, IN 46214
(800) 428-7267

Sams offers an impressive selection of service documentation, including their famous "Sams Photofacts." They may have schematics and service documentation for your printer.

Lee Products Company
800 East 80th St.
Minneapolis, MN 55420

Lee is the manufacturer of "Clean-A-Platen" (product # 10260) used to clean and rejuvenate typewriter and printer platens.

Mill Electronics, Inc.
2026 McDonald Ave.
Brooklyn, NY 11223
(800) 346-8994
(718) 336-4575

Mill stocks electronic components and subassemblies for commercial electronic products.

NTE Electronics, Inc.
44 Farrand St.
Bloomfield, NJ 07003
(800) 631-1250

NTE provides a comprehensive selection of active and passive electronic devices including many foreign components.

Stanford Corporation
Bellwood, IL 60104
Stanford produces "Solvene" (Cat # 00078) used to clean and rejuvenate typewriter and printer platens.

Union Electronic Distributors
16012 So. Cottage Grove
So. Holland, IL 60473
(800) 648-6657
(708) 333-4100
UED stocks electronic replacement parts.

Glossary

ACK Acknowledge. A handshaking signal sent from printer to computer indicating that the printer has successfully received a character.

anode The positive electrode of a two-terminal electronic device.

ASCII American Standard Code for Information Interchange. A standard set of binary codes that define basic letters, numbers, and symbols.

auto feed A rarely used signal from the computer that allows the printer to automatically advance paper upon receiving a carriage return <CR> character.

base One of three electrodes on a bipolar transistor.

baud rate The rate of serial data transmissions which is measured in bits per second (bps).

binary A number system consisting of only two digits.

busy A handshaking signal sent from printer to computer indicating that the printer cannot accept any more characters.

capacitance The measure of a device's ability to store an electric charge, measured in farads, microfarads, or picofarads.

capacitor A device used to store an electrical charge.

cathode The negative electrode of a two terminal electronic device.

collector One of three electrodes on a bipolar transistor.

continuity The integrity of a connection measured as a very low resistance by an ohmmeter.

corona A field of concentrated electrical charge produced by a large voltage potential. Corona wires form one electrode of this voltage potential.

cpi Characters per inch. The number of characters that will fit onto one inch of horizontal line space, also called character pitch.

cpl   Characters per line. The number of characters that will fit on a single horizontal line.

cps   Characters per second. The rate at which characters are delivered to the page surface by a printer.

CTS   Clear to send. A serial handshaking line at the computer usually connected to the RTS line of a printer.

data   Any of eight parallel data lines that carry binary information from computer to printer.

data buffer   Temporary memory where characters from the computer are stored by the printer prior to printing.

DCD   Data carrier defect. A serial handshaking line usually found in serial modem interfaces.

diode   A two-terminal electronic device used to conduct current in one direction only.

driver   An amplifier used to convert low-power signals into high-power signals.

DSR   Data set ready.   The primary computer signal line for hardware handshaking over a serial interface. It is connected to the DTR line at the printer.

DTR   Data terminal ready. The primary serial printer signal for hardware handshaking over a serial interface. It is connected to the DSR pin at the computer.

emitter   One of three electrodes on a bipolar transistor.

encoder   An electro-optical device used to relay the speed and direction of the print head back to main logic.

EPROM   Eraseable programmable read only memory. An advanced type of permanent memory that can be erased and re-written to many times.

font   A character set of particular size, style, and spacing.

gates   Integrated circuits used to perform simple logical operations on binary data in digital systems.

GND   Ground. A common electrical reference point for electronic data signals.

inductance   The measure of a device's ability to store a magnetic charge, measured in henries, millihenries, or microhenries.

inductor   A device used to store a magnetic charge.

initialization   Restoring default or start-up conditions to the printer due to fault or power-up.

laser   A device producing a narrow intense beam of coherent, single-wavelength light waves.

lpi   Lines per inch. The number of horizontal lines that fit into one inch of vertical page space, also known as line pitch.

microprocessor   A complex programmable logic device that will perform various logical operations and calculations based on pre-determined program instructions.

motor   An electromechanical device used to convert electrical energy into mechanical motion.

MTBF   Mean time between failures. A measure of a device's reliability expressed as time or an amount of use.

multimeter   A versatile test instrument used to test such circuit parameters as voltage, current, and resistance.

NLQ Near letter quality. High-quality dot-matrix characters formed with high-density print heads, or by making multiple printing passes.

parity An extra bit added to a serial data word used to check for errors in communication.

paper error P.E. A handshaking signal sent from the printer to tell the computer that paper is exhausted.

photosensitive A material or device that reacts electrically when exposed to light.

piezoelectric The property of certain materials to vibrate when voltage is applied to them.

RAM Random access memory. A temporary memory device used to store digital information.

regulator An electronic device used to control the output of voltage and current from a power supply.

resistance The measure of a device's ability to limit electrical current, measured in ohms, kilo-ohms, or mega-ohms.

resistor A device used to limit the flow of electrical current.

ROM Read only memory. A permanent memory device used to store digital information.

RTS Request to send. A printer serial handshaking line usually connected to the CTS line of a computer.

Rx Receive data. This is the serial input line. The printer's Rx line is connected to the computer's Tx line.

select A control signal from the computer that prepares the printer to receive data.

solenoid An electromechanical device consisting of a coil of wire wrapped around a core which is free to move.

strobe A handshaking line from the computer which tells the printer to accept valid parallel data on its data lines.

toner A fine powder of plastic, iron, and pigments used to form images in electrostatic printing systems.

transistor A three terminal electronic device whose output signal is proportional to its input signal. A transistor can act as an amplifier or a switch.

transistor A device used to step the voltage and current levels of ac signals.

Tx Transmit data. This is the data output line for serial devices. The computer's Tx line is connected to the printer's Rx line.

Bibliography

Computer Products, Inc. *Power Supply Engineering Handbook*. Fremont, California: Computer Products, Inc., 1990.

Cook, Rick. "Page Printers." *Byte*, (September, 1987): 187–197.

Greenfield, Joseph D. *Practical Digital Design Using ICs*. New York: John Wiley & Sons, 1983.

Heilborn, John. *Printer Troubleshooting and Repair*. Carmel, Indiana: Howard W. Sams, 1988.

House, Kim G. & Marble, Jeff. *Printer Connections Bible*. Carmel, Indiana: Howard W. Sams, 1985.

Osborne, Adam. *Introduction to Microcomputers* (Volume 1, 2nd. Ed.). Berkeley: Osborne/McGraw Hill, 1980.

Pasahow, Edward J. *Microprocessors and Microcomputers for Electronics Technicians*. New York: McGraw-Hill, 1981.

Schuler, Charles A. *Electronics: Principles and Applications*. New York: McGraw-Hill, 1979.

Videojet Systems International, Inc. *The Basics of Better Product Marking and Coding*. Elk Grove Village, Illinois: Videojet Systems International, Inc., 1990.

Index